D0742229

China's Telecommunications Market

ADVANCES IN CHINESE ECONOMIC STUDIES

Series Editor: Yanrui Wu, *Senior Lecturer in Economics, University of Western Australia, Australia*

The Chinese economy has been transformed dramatically in recent years. With its rapid economic growth and accession to the World Trade Organisation, China is emerging as an economic superpower. China's development experience provides valuable lessons to many countries in transition.

Advances in Chinese Economic Studies aims, as a series, to publish the best work on the Chinese economy by economists and other researchers throughout the world. It is intended to serve a wide readership including academics, students, business economists and other practitioners.

Titles in the series include:

The Evolution of the Stock Market in China's Transitional Economy
Chien-Hsun Chen and Hui-Tzu Shih

Financial Reform and Economic Development in China
James Laurenceson and Joseph C.H. Chai

China's Telecommunications Market
Entering a New Competitive Age
Ding Lu and Chee Kong Wong

Banking and Insurance in the New China
Competition and the Challenge of Accession to the WTO
Chien-Hsun Chen and Hui-Tzu Shih

China's Telecommunications Market

Entering a New Competitive Age

by

Ding Lu

Associate Professor of Economics, National University of Singapore

Chee Kong Wong

PhD Candidate for Economics, University of Western Australia

ADVANCES IN CHINESE ECONOMIC STUDIES

Edward Elgar
Cheltenham, UK • Northampton, MA, USA

Published by
Edward Elgar Publishing Limited
Glensanda House
Montpellier Parade
Cheltenham
Glos GL50 1UA
UK

Edward Elgar Publishing, Inc.
136 West Street
Suite 202
Northampton
Massachusetts 01060
USA

A catalogue record for this book
is available from the British Library

Library of Congress Cataloguing in Publication Data

Lu, Ding, 1957-
  China's telecommunications market : entering a new competitive age / Ding Lu
and Chee Kong Wong.
    p. cm. — (Advances in Chinese economic studies)
  Includes bibliographical references and index.
    1. Telecommunication—China. I. Wong, Chee Kong. II. Title. III. Series.

  HE8424.L78 2004
  384'.041'0951—dc21

                                                                    2003049265
  ISBN 1 84064 431 1

Printed and bound in Great Britain by MPG Books Ltd, Bodmin, Cornwall

To our motherland

Contents

Figures

Tables

Acronyms

3G	the third generation (mobile communications technology)
ARPU	average revenue per user
BOT	build-operate-transfer
BREW	Binary Runtime Environment for Wireless
CATV	community antenna television
CCF	China-China-Foreign
CDMA	code division multiple access
CITIC	China International Trust and Investment Corporation
CNC	China Netcom Corporation Ltd
CPC	Communist Party of China
DGP	Directorate General of Posts
DGT	Directorate General of Telecommunications
DII-SC	department in charge of the information industry under the State Council
FCC	Federal Communications Commission
FDI	foreign direct investment
FI	Foreign investors
FYP	Five-year Plan
GDP	gross domestic product
GNI	gross national income
GNP	gross national product
GPRS	general packet radio service
GSM	global system for mobile communications
ICP	Internet content provider
IDD	international direct dial
IP	Internet protocol
IPO	initial public offering
ISDN	integrated services digital network
ISP	Internet Service Provider
IT	information technology
ITU	International Telecommunications Union
JCSEI	Joint Conference on State Economic Informatization
LATA	local access and transport area
MEI	Ministry of Electronic Industry

MFN	Most Favoured Nation
MII	Ministry of Information Industry
MOFTEC	Ministry of Foreign Trade and Economic Co-operation
MOR	Ministry of Railway
MPT	Ministry of Post and Telecommunications
MRFT	Ministry of Radio, Film, and Television
NAI	Network Access Identifier
NAL	Network Access Licence
NIISC	National Information Infrastructure Steering Committee
NPC	National People's Congress
PCB	provincial communications bureau
PHS	personal handyphone system
PLA	People's Liberation Army
PRC	People's Republic of China
PTA	post and telecom administration
PTB	bureau of post and telecom
PTE	post and telecom enterprise
PTT	post, telephone and telegraph
RMB	*renminbi* (Chinese currency unit, equivalent to *yuan*)
SAR	Special Administrative Region
SARFT	State Administration of Radio, Film and Television
SDPC	State Development and Planning Commission
SLGI	State Leading Group for Informatization
SOE	state-owned enterprise
SPC	State Planning Commission
SSTC	State Science and Technology Commission
TACS	total access communications system
TUT	technical upgrading and transformation
TV	television
VAN	value-added network
VSAT	very small aperture terminal
WAP	wireless application protocol
WiFi	wireless fidelity
WTO	World Trade Organization

Exchange rates

Average (official) exchange rate of foreign currencies for RMB (*Yuan*)

Year	RMB per 100 US Dollar	RMB per 100 Japanese Yen
1985	293.68	1.23
1986	345.28	2.05
1987	372.20	2.57
1988	372.20	2.90
1989	376.50	2.73
1990	478.31	3.30
1991	532.35	3.95
1992	551.47	4.35
1993	576.19	5.18
1994	861.88	8.43
1995	835.17	8.88
1996	831.43	7.64
1997	828.98	6.85
1998	827.90	6.32
1999	827.82	7.27
2000	827.84	7.68
2001	827.72	6.81
2002	828.00	6.57

Note: RMB has been convertible on current account transactions since 1994.

Preface and acknowledgements

A few years ago, after completing a study on China's telecommunications infrastructure development (Lu, 2000), I decided to write a book that could provide a more comprehensive description and in-depth analysis of the regulatory framework and institutional features of the telecommunications market of the most populous nation on earth. Since then the plan has been postponed and delayed repeatedly as I was trying to catch up with the endless institutional and regulatory restructures that have occurred with dazzling speed and sometimes with surprising twists. Finally I reached the conclusion that, in China's political-economic context, institutional dynamics is a norm and any attempt to describe this fluid institutional-regulatory framework as an 'equilibrium' would be in vain. What I can present to the reader of this book are not the features of an established framework but changes after changes in an evolving system. I wish that the accounts and analyses in this book could provide the reader with a vision for identifying the forces of change in this dynamic industry, a basis for comprehending the unfolding events in this unique regulatory regime, and a map for finding business opportunities in this fast-growing market.

In preparation for this book, I had the fortune to combine the process of material collection and data analysis with my supervision of Chee Kong Wong on writing his thesis for the degree of Master of Social Science at the National University of Singapore (Wong, 2002). As a hardworking and detail-oriented student, Chee Kong provided effective research assistance and served as a helpful coauthor in this project by collecting useful information, helping on statistical analysis, and preparing the final prints. I wish him all the best for his continuous academic pursuit in the University of Western Australia.

I am deeply indebted to Gao Yangzhi, Shen Guanghui and others at the Shanghai Institute of Post and Telecommunications Economics for their valuable support in data collection. In particular, Mr Gao's experience, knowledge and insight guided me into understanding the 'Chinese characteristics' of this fascinating industry.

This book also greatly benefited from the discussion with the audience of my seminar on China's telecom industry presented at the East Asian Institute of the National University of Singapore in February 2001. Comments from Wang Gungwu, John Wong, Tian Xiaowen, Kong Qingjiang and others at the

Institute were particularly helpful. In addition, the excellent collections in the library of the Institute were a big boost to our work. We are grateful to the librarians for their services.

We thank Edward Elgar for offering us this opportunity to publish our work. We are thankful to Alexandra Minton, Nep Athwal, Joanne Broom, Alison Stone, Caroline McLin and Emma Meldrum for their patience and professional support that have made the publication of this book possible.

Last but not least, I want to thank Qing, my wife, for her continuous and persistent support in my academic pursuit.

Ding Lu
June 2003

Foreword

I once visited Fudan University in Shanghai. It was in the autumn of 1988 and I was asked to give four-week lectures on economics of information. Before leaving Japan, I was warned that calling home from China would be difficult. It really was. In fact, it was not easy even to reach a city operator for placing an international call and I gave up after a few futile attempts.

What amazing progress we see today in China! Everywhere in city streets, you see people talking on mobile telephones. Broadband access to the Internet is no longer a dream to the country's millions of '*netizens*'(Internet users). Telecommunications is now a locomotive of the gigantic and dynamic Chinese economy advancing from backwardness towards modernity.

This book is a systematic and comprehensive account of the changes in China's telecom sector for the period from the late 1970s to 2003. The authors, Dr Ding Lu and his student Mr Chee Kong Wong, have summarized its rich recent history into six chapters, each concentrating on interesting topics.

The reader will see, in the first chapter, that China's telecom sector has been an 'overachiever' in the fast-growing Chinese economy. The authors then explain the process in which the old-style government-run telecom sector, 'an ugly duck', was transformed into a dynamic market with several competing carriers. Of particular interest is the way in which two opposing elements, decentralization (driven by regional and local interests) and centralization (driven by the need to exploit network efficiency), coexisted side by side in China's telecom sector throughout the process of its transformation and growth. The reader may also appreciate the 'Chinese way' of introducing competition: it is an outcome from power conflicts among the 'governing' State Council, the lower-level entities such as the ministries of various domains and the regional authorities.

The book includes a chapter explaining some of the initial impacts of China's accession to the World Trade Organization (WTO) in the autumn of 2001. China definitely needs foreign capital and technology for rapid growth, but would like to have them without giving up too much 'creams' (industrial revenues) to outsiders. We have thus seen a gradual and reluctant opening of China's telecom market. The book ends with a chapter featuring the present state of China's telecom sector and giving the prospects that the information technology (IT) industry will continue to be the Chinese economy's 'foundation, pioneer and pillar' in the government's development agenda for the coming years.

I enjoyed, and also learned, a great deal by reading the manuscript of this book. It provides the reader with a detailed but well-organized description of an extremely complicated subject, the evolution of China's telecom sector. It offers a clear perspective of the political economic forces at work in this process. It describes China's telecom sector in light of a global trend towards competition and it does so based on observations of what actually have taken place in China. It uses statistical analysis to an extent necessary for presentation. It is an honest scholarly work in that the source of information is provided in detail. Finally, it has three useful appendices: a chronology of China's telecom industry and two regulations on the industry and foreign businesses.

The book should be useful and enjoyable to scholars, students and government officials, who are interested in the development of China's telecom sector, as well as to business practitioners who are keen to enter this dynamic telecommunications market.

Hajime Oniki
Osaka-Gakuin University, Japan

1. A great leap forward to the information age

A remarkable development that has occurred at the turn of the century has been the emergence of the People's Republic of China (PRC) as the world's largest telephone subscriber base. Starting as a lacklustre monopoly featured by poor-quality service and inadequate capacity, China's telecommunications (telecom) sector has, in a period of merely a dozen years, successfully transformed itself into a dynamic industry boasting a state-of-the-art communications network that promises enormous potentials for competition. The landscape of the world telecom market has since been totally changed.

1.1 THE EXPLOSIVE GROWTH

Twenty years ago, when China[1] launched itself into an unprecedented phase of rapid economic growth, the telecom sector was one of the worst bottlenecks in the economy. The number of telephone terminals per 100 residents was only 0.43 in 1980. Most of the rural residents, which accounted for over 80 per cent of total population, had no access to a telephone service at all. Those lucky enough to have it had to share a single line among households in the whole village. Even in cities and towns, owning a residential telephone terminal was a rare luxury preserved only for the privileged high-ranking officials. The rest had to share one community phone line among dozens or even hundreds of households. Supply was not only short in quantity but also poor in quality. A caller often had to wait more than one minute before getting a dial tone. A wait of similar length was also likely before the call could be connected after the number was dialled.

This situation caused grave concerns to the policy makers. In 1984, the State Council[2] acknowledged that the sector was 'seriously backward' and there existed a 'remarkable gap between supply and demand'.[3] The government then introduced policy stimuli and a series of reforms to the industry, speeding up development of telecom infrastructure in the mid-1980s to meet the booming market demand.

Since then the telecom sector has possessed a strategic spot in China's industrial policy regime. The average growth rate of main telephone lines from 1988 to 1991 doubled the rate of gross domestic product (GDP) growth and accelerated above 30 per cent after 1992. Throughout the 1990s the growth rate of telephone lines consistently exceeded that of GDP, on average three to four times higher (Figure 1.1). Considering that China has been one of the world's fastest-growing economies that has chalked up a GDP growth rate of over 9 per cent per annum during this period, the rapid growth of its telecom network capacity is truly a miracle on top of a miracle.

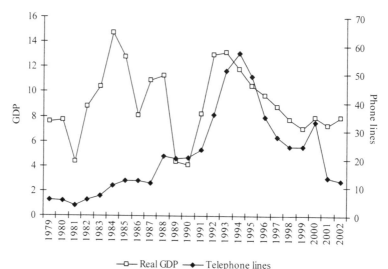

Source: China Statistical Yearbook and *Yearbook of China Transportation and Communications*, various issues, Beijing; Euromonitor from International Telecommunications Union/national statistical offices.

Figure 1.1   *Annual percentage growth rates of real GDP and number of fixed-line phone subscribers (1979–2002)*

Table 1.1 shows that the development of China's telecom sector has gone well beyond its central planners' expectation. Again and again the explosive growth of the industry has made a mockery of government forecasts. Take the switchboard capacity for example. Capacity building was overshot by 25 per cent during the Sixth Five-year Plan period (1981–85) and by 30 per cent during the Seventh Five-year Plan period (1986–90).

Table 1.1   *Telecommunications infrastructure development: planned and achieved (1981–2000)*

Five-year Plan Period (target to be achieved by the end of the period)		6th FYP 1981– 1985	7th FYP 1986– 1990	8th FYP 1991– 1995	9th FYP 1996– 2000
Local switchboard capacity (million lines)	Planned	2.70	6.35	18.0	150
	Achieved	3.37	8.26	54.6	179
Long-distance phone lines (thousand)	Planned	28.01	109.62	350.00	2,800.00
	Achieved	37.55	112.44	735.55	5,635.50
Telephone terminals per 100 residents (up from 0.43 in 1980)	Planned	N/A	N/A	Above 2.0	10.0 (urban: 30–40)
	Achieved	0.6	1.11	4.66	20.1 (urban: 39)
Total phone terminals (million)	Planned	N/A	9.5	23.9	123.0
	Achieved	6.3	12.7	57.6	171.5
Of which: mobile phones (million)	Planned	N/A	N/A	N/A	18.0
	Achieved	N/A	0.02	3.63	84.5
Post-telecom turnover growth rate per annum	Planned	5.0%	11.1%	20.0%	20.0%
	Achieved	9.8%	22.5%	35.1%	38.0%

Note: Figures are of the end of the period except for the growth rates.

Source: *Yearbook of China Transportation and Communications*, various issues, Beijing; Ministry of Information Industry website, http://www.mii.gov.cn/.

Table 1.2   Local switchboard capacity in China (1978–2002)

Year	Local switchboard capacity	
	Million lines	**% change**
1978	4.059	
1979	4.220	3.97
1980	4.432	5.02
1981	4.634	4.56
1982	4.907	5.89
1983	5.161	5.18
1984	5.536	7.27
1985	6.134	10.80
1986	6.724	9.62
1987	7.739	15.10
1988	8.872	14.64
1989	10.347	16.63
1990	12.318	19.05
1991	14.922	21.14
1992	19.151	28.34
1993	30.408	58.78
1994	49.262	62.00
1995	72.036	46.23
1996	92.912	28.98
1997	112.692	21.29
1998	138.237	22.67
1999	158.531	14.68
2000	178.256	16.16
2001	205.695	15.37
2002	283.584	37.86

Source: *China Statistical Yearbook* and *Yearbook of China Transportation and Communications*, various issues, Beijing; Ministry of Information Industry website, http://www.mii.gov.cn/.

In 1995 the capacity hit 200 per cent higher than what was specified in the Eighth Plan period (1991–95)! Only in the first half of the 1990s, China installed more than 73 million phone lines, more than all the rest of the developing world combined. Switchboard capacity leaped from four million lines prior to 1985 to 179 million by the end of 2000 (see Table 1.2). The number of fixed-line phone subscribers increased from two million in 1979 to 214 million by the end of 2002 (see Table 1.3). In the first decade of this century,

China is likely to see fixed-line users increase to somewhere near 300 million or even more.

Table 1.3　　*Number of fixed-line phone subscribers in China (1978–2002)*

Year	Fixed-line phone subscribers	
	Number of subscribers (million)	% change
1978	1.925	
1979	2.033	5.61
1980	2.141	5.31
1981	2.221	3.74
1982	2.343	5.49
1983	2.508	7.04
1984	2.775	10.65
1985	3.120	12.43
1986	3.504	12.31
1987	3.907	11.50
1988	4.727	20.99
1989	5.680	20.16
1990	6.850	20.60
1991	8.451	23.37
1992	11.469	35.71
1993	17.332	51.12
1994	27.295	57.48
1995	40.706	49.13
1996	54.947	34.99
1997	70.310	27.96
1998	87.421	24.34
1999	108.716	24.36
2000	144.829	33.22
2001	180.368	24.50
2002	214.419	18.88

Source:　　*China Statistical Yearbook* and *Yearbook of China Transportation and Communications*, various issues, Beijing; Ministry of Information Industry website, http://www.mii.gov.cn/.

Since the mid-1990s, China's telecom market expansion has also been driven by the emergence and rapid expansion of its mobile network (see Table 1.4). The growth again went beyond industrial planners' expectations. At the end of 1999, the Ministry of Information Industry (MII) anticipated that the total number of mobile phone subscribers would increase to 70 million a year later.[4] The project was already almost four times of what was planned for in the Ninth Five-year Plan (see Table 1.1). The result was nevertheless an even higher 84.5 million. It was also projected by the end of 1999 that a further 100 million mobile phone subscribers would be added by 2003 and another 200 million by 2010.[5]

Table 1.4   Number of mobile phone subscribers in China (1988–2002)

Year	Mobile phone subscribers	
	No. of subscribers (million)	% change
1988	0.003	
1989	0.010	206.25
1990	0.018	86.73
1991	0.048	159.56
1992	0.177	272.63
1993	0.639	261.01
1994	1.568	145.38
1995	3.629	131.44
1996	6.853	88.84
1997	13.233	93.10
1998	23.863	80.33
1999	43.238	81.20
2000	84.533	95.51
2001	145.222	71.80
2002	206.616	42.27

Source: *China Statistical Yearbook* and *Yearbook of China Transportation and Communications*, various issues, Beijing; Ministry of Information Industry website, http://www.mii.gov.cn/.

By December 2002, the number of mobile phone subscribers had already surpassed 200 million. Symbolic of the huge changes in this sector is the length of China's mobile phone number growing to 11 digits by July 1999. Such an increase amplifies the mobile phone number capacity from 50 million to about 500 million, which should meet the country's demand by 2010.[6]

After a 15-year period of hyper growth, China now boasts the world's largest telephone subscriber base. In 1985, China's telephone network was ranked 17th in the world. Only 12 years later in 1997, it became the world's second largest.[7] By July 2001 the number of China's mobile telephone users reached 120.6 million, surpassing that of the US and making China the world's largest mobile telephone market. China overtook the US in March 2002 as the world's largest telephone network both in terms of capacity and subscriber base, with 190 million fixed-line subscribers and 160 million mobile phone subscribers. Transmission of both the fixed-line network and the mobile network has been digitalized. The total telephone customer base was 87 times that of 1978, the year when China launched the market-oriented reform.[8]

Table 1.5   Penetration rate and teledensity in China (1985–2002)

Year	Penetration rate	Teledensity
1985	0.60	
1986	0.67	
1987	0.75	
1988	0.86	
1989	0.98	
1990	1.11	
1991	1.29	
1992	1.61	
1993	2.20	
1994	3.20	
1995	4.66	3.36
1996	6.33	4.49
1997	8.11	5.68
1998	10.53	7.00
1999	13.00	8.64
2000	20.10	11.45
2001	25.90	14.14
2002	33.74	16.80

Note: Penetration rate is the number of telephone terminals per 100 residents; teledensity is the number of telephone main lines per 100 residents.

Source: *China Statistical Yearbook* and *Yearbook of China Transportation and Communications*, various issues, Beijing; Ministry of Information Industry website, http://www.mii.gov.cn/.

1.2   CATCHING UP WITH THE WORLD

As a result of the market expansion, the telephone penetration rate (measured by the number of telephone terminals per 100 persons) rose sharply from 0.6 per cent in 1985 to 1.1 per cent in 1990, and to 20.1 per cent in 2000. In urban areas, the rate reached 17 per cent by 1995 and over 39 per cent by 2000. Many coastal cities, in particular, had raised their telephone penetration level from less than 3 per cent to above 30 per cent by 1995 in less than a decade's time. Teledensity (measured by main telephone lines per 100 residents) reached 11.45 per cent in 2000 and 16.80 per cent in 2002 (Table 1.5).

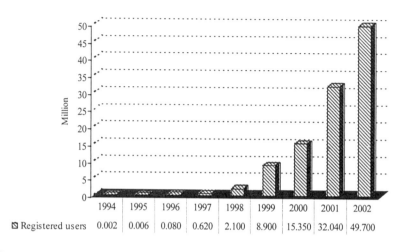

	1994	1995	1996	1997	1998	1999	2000	2001	2002
Registered users	0.002	0.006	0.080	0.620	2.100	8.900	15.350	32.040	49.700

Source: Wong   and   Nah   (2000);   Ministry   of   Information   Industry   website, http://www.mii.gov.cn/.

Figure 1.2   Growth of Internet subscribers (1994–2002)

China's leapfrog into the information age is highlighted by the exponential growth of its '*netizen*' (Internet-user) population since 1994 (Figure 1.2). With approximately 50 million registered Internet subscribers by the end of 2002, China may already have one of the world's largest *netizen* population since Internet account sharing is widespread and thousands of Internet bars host numerous unregistered Internet surfers. In recent years, the quality of the Internet service has improved remarkably. For instance, in 2001 alone, China Telecom trebled its Internet bandwidth for its international gateways and increased the bandwidth for the domestic Internet service by 16 times.[9] It was projected by the Ministry of Information Industry that, by 2005, the total number of China's telephone subscribers would reach 500 million with a telephone penetration rate of 40 per cent and a share of *netizens* in total population of over 15 per cent.[10]

By international comparison, China has been remarkably successful in catching up with the rest of the world in raising its teledensity. As shown in

Figure 1.3, the middle-income country's average teledensity was 13 times higher than China's in 1987 but the gap closed up quickly in the following decade to a difference of only about 20 per cent by 2000. Meanwhile, China strode well ahead of low-income countries in telecom development by reaching a teledensity level five times of the average among the low-income group by the turn of the century (Figure 1.3).

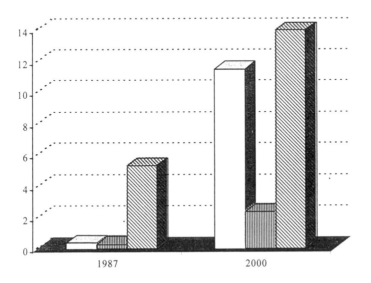

□ China ▥ Low-income country average ◩ Middle-income country average

Note: According to the World Bank classification, countries with per capita gross national income (GNI) below US$ 500 in 1987 or with per capita GNI below US$ $755 or less in 2000 are low-income countries. The per capita GNI range for middle-income countries is US$ 500–6,000 for the year 1987 while the range is US$ 756– 9,265 for the year 2000. China's per capita GNI was US$ 290 in 1987 and US$ 840 in 2000.

Source: Yearbook *of China Transportation and Communications 1991, ITU Yearbook of Statistics 1995, 2001,* and World Bank website, http://www.worldbank.org/data/.

Figure 1.3   *Catching up in teledensity (main telephone lines per 100 residents)*

In a more rigorous way of evaluating the catching-up effect, we first statistically examine the correspondence between teledensity and GNP per capita for low- and middle-income countries as defined by the World Bank. This is based on the underlined assumption of a positive correspondence between the two variables (Lu, 2000). We then used the estimated models to project China's teledensity levels corresponding to its per capita GNP for the years concerned. A comparison between these projected levels and the actual teledensity reveals whether China achieved proper levels of telecom development in these years.

Using the data of 1987 (89 observations) and 2000 (109 observations), we estimated the following equation by regressing the logarithmic values of the teledensity data (LNTELDEN) on the logarithmic values of per capita GDP (LNPCGDP) data:[11]

$$\text{LNTELDEN}_{it} = \alpha + \beta \cdot \text{LNPCGDP}_{it} + \varepsilon_{it}$$

where α is intercept and ε_{it} the error term for sample i at time t. This gives the following results in Table 1.6. The estimated coefficients in both years have a statistical significance of over 99 per cent and both regressions have an R^2 of 0.82.

Table 1.6   Teledensity and per capita GDP (purchasing power parity–adjusted) regression results

Estimates (t-statistics in brackets)	1987	2000
α	−10.9312 (−19.1636)	−9.5074 (−19.6754)
β	1.4722 (19.9646)	1.3497 (22.7753)
R^2	0.8208	0.8290
Adjusted R^2	0.8188	0.8274
Observations	89	109

Table 1.7 shows the results of using the estimated models to project China's teledensity levels corresponding to the country's per capita GDP for the years 1987 and 2000. In 1987, China had a purchasing-power-parity adjusted per capita GDP of US\$ 1136 and a teledensity figure of 0.35, which was about 65 per cent of its forecast level (0.54). By 2000, however, with a purchasing-power-parity adjusted per capita GDP of US\$ 3928, China had reached a teledensity level of 11.33, which was twice the forecast level (5.27). This evidence shows that, between 1987 and 2000, in correspondence to its per capita income, China rose from a below-average achiever to an overachiever in telecommunications development.

Table 1.7   China's teledensity: projected versus actual

	1987	2000
Per capita GDP (US$)	1136	3928
Projected teledensity	0.54	5.27
Actual teledensity	0.35	11.33
Ratio between actual and projected values	65%	215%

Note: Teledensity data calculated from this database is the number of phone lines in use per 100 residents.

Source: Compiled and calculated from Global Market Information Database, www.euromonitor.com.

1.3   AN OVERACHIEVER

From the above data, we see that China has in recent years achieved a level of telecom development in advance of other developing countries at a similar income level. An interesting question is whether China has also been an 'overachiever' in efficiency when building up its immense telecom network. In other words, we are curious to find out whether China has used the mammoth investment to increase supply capacity in a cost-effective way.

To examine this issue, we estimate a regression model to evaluate cost-effectiveness of telecom investment to increase telephone lines in the Asia-Pacific region during the period 1988 to 1998, following the methodology in Lu (2000). In this model, the logarithmic values of annual line increase (unit: thousand lines), LOGLINC, is regressed on three variables:

1.   Previous year's logarithmic values of telecommunications investment (unit: million US$), LOGINV;
2.   The relative teledensity in the sample countries, RTELDEN (the individual country's teledensity divided by the average teledensity);
3.   The relative population density, RPOPDEN (the individual country's population density divided by the average density).

$$\text{LOGLINC}_{it} = \alpha + \beta_1 \text{ LOGINV}_{it-1} + \beta_2 \text{ RTELDEN}_{it} + \beta_3 \text{ RPOPDEN}_i + \varepsilon_{it}$$

Note that according to the ITU definition, investment refers to expenditure associated with acquiring the ownership of telecom equipment infrastructure (including supporting land and buildings and intellectual and non-tangible property such as computer software). These include expenditure on initial installations and on additions to existing installations where the usage is expected to be over an extended period of time. Data are gross investment figures, which include cost of land and buildings.

Including RTELDEN in the model is based on the assumption that countries with low teledensity can save capital cost of infrastructure as 'late starters'. They tend to be more efficient in increasing telephone lines than the 'earlier starters'. This is partially because the 'earlier starters' also have to incur a higher replacement cost in investment to upgrade their existing network. The 'late starters' do not have the earlier starters' burdens of replacing the out-of-date facilities and they can apply the latest technologies to build telecom networks. The low teledensity is also associated with low per capita income levels, which in turn may imply lower land cost and labour cost in infrastructure construction. Given these reasons, we expect the coefficient of RTELDEN to be negative.

High population density should have a positive impact on cost-effectiveness of telecom investment. With fixed-line telephony, the connection cost per telephone line in a densely populated area is usually cheaper than in a sparsely populated region. Therefore we expect the coefficient of RPOPDEN to be positive. With the development of wireless telephony, however, the significance of this impact is likely to be weaker.

Table 1.8   Investment effectiveness model regression results

Variable	Estimate	t-statistic
α (intercept)	−0.4147	−3.4219
β_1 (LOGINV)	1.0752	21.1118
β_2 (RTELDEN)	−2.8945	−5.6986
β_3 (RPOPDEN)	0.0382	2.7291
R^2	0.7495	
Adjusted R^2	0.7450	
Observations	170	

Using the data of 17 Asia-Pacific countries (China not included) during 1989–98 from ITU (1995, 2001), we estimated the model's coefficients as shown in Table 1.8. All estimates in the model have a statistical significance of over 99 per cent.

Based on these estimates, we projected China's main telephone line increase and compared it with the actual line increase. The projections are based on two sets of investment data. One is the US$-denominated investment data published by the ITU, deflated by the US producer price index. The other is made on the RMB-denominated investment figures published in the *Yearbook of China Transportation and Communications.* The figures are first deflated by China's price index and then converted to the US dollar with the swap exchange rate for the period up to 1994 and with the official exchange rates after 1994.[12]

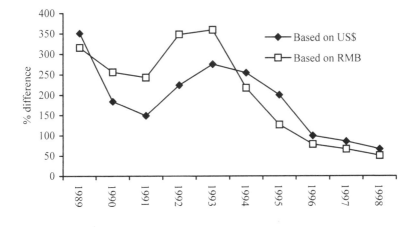

Figure 1.4   Line increase: percentage difference between the projected and the actual

Two observations arise from the comparison between the projected figures and the actual figures (Figure 1.4). One is that, up to 1995, the cost-effectiveness of China's investment in phone lines was 2–4 times higher than the Asia-Pacific average. Such a difference was narrowed after 1995 but still remained above 50 per cent by 1998. This suggests that China telephone network-building has been not only fast but also highly efficient by international comparison. In other words, China has been an overachiever in efficiency as well as in speed. The other observation is the declining trend in the efficiency gap that China has enjoyed.

Several factors may have contributed to China's overachievement. First, the catching-up effect may not have been fully captured by the relative teledensity in our model. In particular, China lacked some crucial market institutions before the mid-1990s, such as a well-developed real estate market, to correctly value the land components in telecom network capital cost. China's labour cost is also relatively low compared to that in other Asia-Pacific economies.

Second, institutional reforms within the telecom sector, which we discuss in detail in the next chapter, could have stimulated labour productivity growth from a relatively low wage base. Meanwhile, as we note later, the state-owned post and telecom enterprises behaved like output/revenue maximizers who did all they could to expand supply capacity. Investment costs and risks involving purchase of new and expensive equipment were minimum or external to them. All this might have encouraged them to employ and import whatever technology that would be most effective and efficient in increasing supply capacity (number of main lines).

Third, the state industrial policies (to be discussed later) were especially favourable to telecom development during the period under study. Thanks to these policies, the telecom sector has faced low barriers to equipment trade and a competitive domestic equipment supply. Open and hidden subsidies could also have contributed to the apparent overachievements to some extent.

Finally, before 1997 the Ministry of Post and Telecommunications (MPT) was both a regulator and a monopoly operator of telecom business. This status empowered the MPT the ability to enforce unified planning of network development. Despite some reports of connection problems between the MPT's public network and some non-public networks owned by several non-MPT departments, the unified MPT standard was effectively enforced nationwide. This may have helped China avoid the costs arising from incompatibility of different network standards.

The narrowing efficiency gap after 1995 confirms some of the above explanations of China's overachievement.

1.   The launch of China's real estate market after 1992 took effect on the price for land uses which thereafter reflected better its market value (or marginal productivity). In many coastal cities, the actual land costs are no longer cheap by international comparison.

2.   The explosive growth of mobile telephony in the late 1990s considerably reduced China's comparative advantages in relative low costs of land and labour inputs in telecom network construction. This is because the investment in a mobile telephone network is less sensitive than the fixed-line network to land cost and labour cost, despite the fact that mobile phone usage also takes on main-line capacity at local exchanges. When the mobile phone's proportion of total phone subscription rises, the main-line construction cost includes smaller contents of land and labour inputs.

3.   The law of diminishing returns has set in for China's catching-up process. One particular aspect relates to population density. Note that the population density data used in our model reflects the national average. In early years of network construction, telephone lines tended to be laid in more densely populated areas where per line construction cost was much lower. When network construction expanded to less densely populated regions, the construction cost had to rise.

4.   Introduction of competition since 1997 has ended MPT and its business descendant China Telecom's monopoly command over network construction. Meanwhile, with further enterprise reforms, Chinese telecom carriers have become more profit-oriented and no longer behave like the output/revenue maximizing post and telecom enterprises of the early days. All these have changed the institutional environment of telecom network development.

Summary

Growth of China's telecom industry in the last two decades has been extraordinary: It not only outperformed most other developing countries but also overshot China's own, already ambitious, plans. The rise of China as the world's largest telecom subscriber base has changed the industrial landscape of the world telecom market.

NOTES

1.   If not otherwise stated, the word 'China' in this book refers to the mainland area under the direct administration of the People's Republic of China.
2.   The State Council, appointed by the National People's Congress, is the cabinet of the PRC government.
3.   Yearbook of China Transportation and Communications 1986, Beijing, p. 243.
4.   *Mingbao* (Hong Kong), 14 January 2000.
5.   *South China Morning Post* (Hong Kong), 20 December 1999.
6.   *China Daily* (Hong Kong), 22 July 1999.
7.   *Far Eastern Economic Review* (Hong Kong), 30 September 1999.
8.   *MII News* 'Telecommunications Becomes One of the Fastest Growing Sectors in China' and 'Speech on the 34th World Telecom Day Symposium' by Zhang Chun Jiang, deputy minister of Ministry of Information Industry, MII website, http://www.mii.gov.cn/, 16 May 2002 and 17 May 2002.
9.   Ministry of Information Industry, *Year 2001 Statistical Communiqué of Communications Industries* (1 April 2002), http://www.mii.gov.cn/.
10.   *Lianhe Zaobao* (United Morning Post, Singapore), 30 May 2002.
11.   We use purchasing-power-parity adjusted GDP for the exercise because nominal per capita GDP tends to underestimate the purchasing power of China's real per capita income and thence exaggerate the extent of overachievement of China's telecom development.

12.   Before 1994, China had a dual-track exchange rate system that operated
      with two types of exchange rate: the official exchange rate and the swap
      exchange rate. The official rate, a legacy of the centrally planned
      system, severely overvalued RMB. The swap rate was the average daily
      trading rate at the few foreign exchange swap centres set up in coastal
      cities in 1988. In 1994, the dual exchange rate system gave way to a
      single exchange rate based on trading results at a unified national
      foreign exchange market (Lin et al., 1996).

2. Behind the hyper growth

China's telecommunications (telecom) sector developed in leaps and bounds after the mid-1980s largely thanks to a series of institutional changes and strong centrally planned initiatives that took place in the 1980s and the 1990s. These developments fundamentally changed the incentive structure of telecom enterprises and their business environment. This supply-side overhaul allowed the industry to meet the rising demand for telecom services fuelled by a rapidly growing economy.

2.1   INITIAL CONDITIONS

When the People's Republic of China (PRC) was founded in 1949, the country of over 500 million people had only 263,000 telephones in the cities with a switchboard capacity of 310,000 lines. Teledensity was only 0.05 (Zhou, 1997). Other than some counties in the coastal provinces, more than 90 per cent of counties in China had no telecom facilities at all (Deng et al., 1993).

For more than two-thirds of the PRC's five-decade-long history, however, development of the telecom sector had tailed the growth of the national economy. As shown in Figure 2.1, telephone local switchboard capacity growth only outpaced the growth of the economy briefly during the period 1957–62 , when the disastrous 'Great Leap Forward' and 'People's Communes' campaigns pushed the economy into the worst recession in the PRC's history.[1] All through the period 1962–85, the growth of telephone switchboard capacity lagged behind the economic growth. While the size of the economy multiplied 6.5 times in real terms, the switchboard capacity increased to only 2.5 times of the base-year level.

As a result, towards the end of the Cultural Revolution, in 1975, China's total switchboard capacity was 3.48 million lines, with teledensity at only 0.35 (Zhou, 1997). Even in 1984, the State Council acknowledged that the sector was 'seriously backward' and there existed a 'remarkable gap between supply and demand'.[2] Relative to the level of 1962, the switchboard capacity expansion could not keep up with the accumulated growth of gross domestic product (GDP) until the early 1990s.

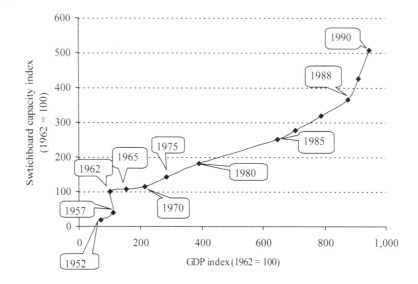

Source: *China Statistical Yearbook* and *Yearbook of China's Transportation and Communications*, various issues, Beijing.

Figure 2.1   GDP index versus switchboard capacity index (1952–1990)

The snail-pace growth was largely due to the low priority given to the telecom sector in the heavy-industry-oriented development plans during the Mao era (1950s to 1970s). The telecom service was seen purely as an instrument of state administrative apparatus or as part of the national defence and security system. As for residential telephony, the service was an exclusive political privilege reserved for high-ranking officials only. While residential telephony was regarded as a luxury, provision of universal services to the non-privileged mass was never on the agenda. The civil telecom service was perceived by the central planners as 'non-productive' and was therefore a typical 'buffer sector' in a centrally planned economy, which from time to time had to give way to sectors that received higher priorities. Consequently, planned investment in the civil telecom sector was often diverted to other needs (Yang, 1991; Gao, 1991). Figure 2.2 shows that investment in the postal and telecom sector never exceeded RMB 2 billion during the first Five-year Plans until 1980. Its share in the total state fixed capital investment had always been below 1 per cent before 1985. Capital construction investment even came to a halt in the early 1970s (Figure 2.3).

When China launched its economic modernization programme with market-oriented reforms in the late 1970s, the telecom sector stood as a glaring bottleneck in the economy. This caused serious concerns to the policy makers. Meanwhile, as China gradually opened itself up to the world, the message of a dawning information age spread quickly in the country with the buzzwords of 'The Third Wave' and the 'post-industrial society' (Mueller and Tan, 1997, 14). The Chinese leaders came to realize that 'informatization' was equally as important as 'industrialization' and indispensable to the nation's modernization programme.

Starting in 1979, the government moved to speed up the growth of the post and telecom sector by introducing a series of reforms and policy stimuli. As the government took decisive steps to make the communications sector a priority for development, the sector saw its share in total state investment assume an upward trend in the 6th and 7th Five-year Plan periods (1981–85 and 1986–90) (Figure 2.2).

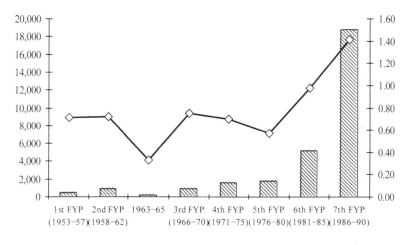

 🖾 Post-telecom investment ─◇─ As % of total state investment

Source: *Yearbook of China's Transportation and Communications,* various issues.

Figure 2.2   *Fixed capital investment in postal and telecom sector (million RMB)*

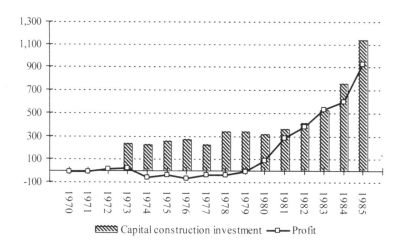

Note: 'Profit' refers to pre-tax profit.

Source: *Yearbook of China Transportation and Communications 1996* and *China Statistical Yearbook*, various issues.

Figure 2.3   *Capital construction investment and profit of postal and telecom enterprises (million RMB)*

2.2   ORGANIZATIONAL REVAMP

The first step was an organizational revamp. In the pre-reform years, due to the 'non-productive' status of the investment, the post and telecom enterprises (PTEs) were considered 'non-profit institutions', granted little incentive to increase revenues or expand businesses. This was reflected in the fact that these enterprises were in the red eight out of the ten years in the 1970s (Figure 2.3). The state-owned telecom sector was placed under a rigid, semi-military administrative structure under the Ministry of Post and Telecommunications (MPT), the functional organ of the State Council responsible for nationwide postal and telecom services.

The MPT pre-reform system was highly centralized with little autonomy and financial accountability at the local enterprise level. All enterprise revenues were collected vertically by the hierarchical authorities along the administrative structure. Expenses were claimed from higher authorities by those low in the hierarchy. The MPT centrally allocated nationwide investment. During the chaotic Cultural Revolution (1966–76), the MPT was once dissolved in 1969 and the telecom sector was put under the regional military administrations. When the MPT was restored in 1973, it was not able to immediately regain centralized control of the national postal and telecom network. From 1973 to 1979, the governments at the levels of province, municipality and prefecture had the actual control over the planning of postal and telecom business in their domains. The fragmented administrative structure caused many coordinating problems in the industry.[3]

In 1979, the State Council issued a directive to make the MPT the dominant central planner of the nationwide post and telecom development. Local PTEs were put under the 'dual leadership' of provincial governments and the MPT, with the latter the main decision maker. Meanwhile administration of the daily business operation was to be decentralized with the introduction of primary financial accountability at the local level. As stipulated by the directive, in this sector, the government administration and business management was supposed to be separated. The postal business and telecom business should also be separately administrated. The enterprises should have their own accounts and would be made financially independent.[4] In line with the above principles, local post and telecom administrations (PTAs) were set up at the provincial level under the 'dual leadership' of the MPT and the provincial governments.

From 1983 to 1985, the MPT introduced a new accounting system, known as 'Enterprise Own Revenue', to define an elaborate methodology for calculating an individual PTE's income (Guo and Xu, 1992; Xu, 1996). By the mid-1980s, all the PTEs had built their independent accounts and started to operate on a system of contractual responsibility in which their earnings were linked to their business performance.[5]

With the reforms to place the local PTEs in a system of contractual responsibility, a vertically organized hierarchy emerged as the administrative structure of China's telecommunications. The national ministry at the top was responsible for overall planning and management of the industry. It controlled international and inter-provincial communications. It also set and enforced technical standards and formulated key policies and plans. At the provincial level, the PTAs performed a similar role within the province. Below them were hundreds of municipal and prefecture bureaus of post and telecom (PTBs). Next, more than 2,000 county-level PTEs operated local service networks in the county capitals and extended lines into the surrounding rural areas. Below them were tens of thousands of branch offices operating exchanges at the village level. There were also many non-public branch exchanges owned and operated by work units and rural villages (Mueller and Tan, 1997).

The MPT system underwent a deeper revamp in 1988 amid a major state-owned enterprise reform initiative taking place nationwide. The MPT granted its national manufacturing, construction and purchasing departments status of separate legal entities or greater independence in financial accounting and human resource management. Meanwhile the MPT set up the Directorate General of Telecommunications (DGT) and the Directorate General of Posts (DGP) to incorporate business enterprise functions.

The DGT comprised 29 provincial PTAs, all of which offered local and long-distance services through the 1990s. The PTAs in Beijing, Shanghai and Guangdong also offered international services. The MPT itself handled regulatory matters through its Department of Policy and Regulation. The MPT's DGT eventually registered with the government as a corporate group, China Telecom, in 1995.[6] Consequently, all the PTEs under China Telecom went through a process of 'corporatization' to restructure themselves into independent accounting entities that conform with the Corporation Law (implemented in 1994). It thus took more than a decade for the MPT regime to go through the process of corporatizing its business operations into a separate spin-off.

2.3   RESTRUCTURING INCENTIVES

Paralleled to organizational reforms, various financial stimuli came to promote the infrastructure development and industrial performance. Traditionally, the MPT centrally controlled the pricing of most services, which included monthly subscription and communication charges. The tariff policy before the 1980s was to underprice telephone services. Upward adjustment of rates was rare. Due to the underpriced rates, before 1980 the postal and telecom sector was in the red for more than ten years.

In October 1984, the State Council gave the green light to upward adjustment of service rates.[7] During the period 1986–90, the MPT made adjustments to a wide range of telecom service rates. Consequently, the rate of capital return in the industry increased from 9 per cent in 1986 to 17 per cent in 1990, much higher than the average rate of capital return for all industries. According to the World Bank, the rate of return of China's telecom industry in 1989, adjusted for accounting differentials, was equivalent to 12 per cent by Western business standards (Ma, 1992). The tariff structure also had a clear cross-subsidizing feature, with the rate of return much lower for local (intra-city) city services and higher for long-distance and international services.[8]

Meanwhile, local telecom companies were authorized to set their own intra-city rates not exceeding a cap set by the MPT according to local telephone companies' average costs with a mark-up for profit. These rate adjustments were subject to the approval of local government's price control authorities (Sun, 1992). By the end of 1990, the intra-city telephone rates had been widely adjusted. The ministry set a price cap.

Along with the above fee adjustments, a system of 'special funding accounts' was adopted to manage the moneys collected by PTEs. The source (credit) side of these accounts consisted of the 'earmarked grants' from the government and the 'specialized funds' which were collected by the enterprises themselves. The proportion of government grants in postal and telecom investment declined sharply from 59 per cent in 1980 to 29 per cent in 1981. It continued to drop down to 10 per cent in 1989. The use (liability) side of these accounts divided funds into specialized purposes such as line maintenance and upgrading, new technology development, and local telephone line constructions and connections. The system ensured that the funds collected (such as installation fees) were used solely for their earmarked purposes (such as line construction).[9]

As for service operation, the accounting reform in the mid-1980s provided the basis to contract performance responsibilities to enterprise managers and employees. Under the reformed accounting rules, apart from keeping the revenue from the local (intra-city) services, each PTE received a share of the accounting-rate-based annual revenue from the inter-regional traffic it had generated. In addition, it also retained a bonus income equivalent to a proportion of the increased (actual) operation revenue over the previous year's basis (Lu, 2000).

In the early 1990s, the accounting rates for calculating the revenue from an enterprise's inter-regional traffic were based on 1987's average cost and profit-tax rate in the industry. A catalogue issued by the MPT lists the accounting rates of more than 140 service products. The share coefficient to determine an enterprise's claim of the accounting revenue from its inter-region service was estimated by regressing the 32 provincial telecom companies' real costs against seven factors such as per capita income, weather condition, telecom infrastructure investment and so on (Zhang, 1991). A net contributing PTE would have a share coefficient less than unity while a net receiving PTE would have one greater than unity.

Based on the above formula, the ministry contracted performance responsibilities to all the local PTEs. By 1995, most PTEs had completed three contracting periods, namely, 1985–88, 1989–91 and 1992–95. The more recent contracts included supplementary evaluative criteria such as communication quality and capital investment. Beginning in 1991, some contracts included terms of 'asset responsibility', which defined the managers' responsibility of maintaining and improving the state assets under their charge (Liu, 1992).

An important incentive incorporated in these contracts was to link PTBs' wage fund increase to their sales revenue increase.[10] How much the employees and managers could actually get paid from the wage fund was determined by a multiplier, of which the value depended on the evaluation of four aspects of performance with different percentage weights: Communication quality (40 per cent); communication quantity (20 per cent); profit level (20 per cent); and labour productivity (20 per cent). In 1994, some other factors, including asset value and wage–profit ratio, were added to the rating in order to encourage greater efficiency.

Such an incentive structure strongly encouraged business expansion. For the PTE employees and managers, the effective way of increasing their wage fund was to increase the revenue of the enterprise and the MPT's national network by generating more telecom traffic. As service prices and tariffs for long-distance communications were set by the MPT and the local rates and installation charges were capped, revenue maximization was equivalent to output maximization.

Before the mid-1990s, given the low teledensity, strong and growing demand, and infrastructure bottleneck, China's telecom market had been a supply-constrained one. The PTEs thus had no alternative but to make all-out efforts to increase their supply capacity by expanding local telecom infrastructure. Such drives met timely state support.

2.4   STATE SUPPORT

From the 1980s to the 1990s, the telecom sector received various financial stimuli from the state. In October 1984, the State Council stipulated a 'six-point instruction' to give priority to postal and telecom development (Gao, 1991). A policy of 'three 90-per cent' was adopted:

- 90 per cent of profit was to be retained by the MPT (in other words, the tax rate is 10 per cent, well below the 55 per cent tax rate for other industries before 1994);
- 90 per cent of foreign exchange (hard currency) earnings were to be retained by the MPT; and
- 90 per cent of central government investment was not considered as repayable loans.

In addition, the PTEs and PTBs also enjoyed favourable interest rates when they borrowed from state banks. The preferential 'three 90-per cent' policy provided favourable conditions for the sector's expansion until the year 1994 when a major fiscal monetary reform unified corporate tax rates, simplified the tax levy structure and made Chinese currency convertible for current account transactions. The policy played a pivotal role in propelling the telecom sector to take off.

In October 1988, the State Council announced the so-called '16-character policy' for telecom infrastructure development (Jin, 1992). The policy was summarized by 16 Chinese characters,[11] which outline four principles:

- Overall planning of industrial development should be unified under the MPT.
- Ministerial administration should be coordinated with regional authorities.
- Responsibilities should be defined and shared among different administrative levels.
- Construction of infrastructure should mobilize resources from all concerned.

Based on these principles, financing postal and telecom investment was largely decentralized in the late 1980s. The Seventh Five-year Plan (1986–90) stipulated that the intra-provincial telecom projects should rely mainly on local financing. Institutions or individuals should be encouraged to contribute to infrastructure investment. Those who had invested in telecom projects could benefit from receiving priority of being connected to the network and lower charges for telecom services. In the rural area, whoever invested in the infrastructure facilities could manage and operate the local exchanges (You, 1987).

An important state policy to facilitate telecom investment was to allow a faster pace of capital depreciation in the postal and telecom sector. The State Council's 'six-point' instruction of 1984 promised to gradually raise the accounting capital depreciation of the postal and telecom sector to 7 per cent.[12] From 1980 to 1990, the government adjusted capital depreciation rate upward three times.[13] A reform of the PTE accounting system in July 1993 again raised the capital depreciation rate.[14] In 1995, the gross fixed capital depreciation rate was as high as 16 per cent. The capital depreciation amounted to RMB 40 billion, accounting for more than 40 per cent of the total fixed capital investment.[15] Capital depreciation was the main source of technical upgrading and transformation (TUT) investment. The higher depreciation rate in the postal and telecom sector led to a higher-than-average weight of TUT investment in total fixed capital investment. Thanks to the policy, from the mid-1980s to the end of the 1990s, the weight of TUT investment in fixed capital investment in the postal and telecom sector increased drastically and was much higher than that prevailing in other state-owned industries (Figure 2.4).

Another important tax policy that favoured telecom sector development in the 1990s was the coordinating tax for directions of fixed capital investment. The tax, introduced in 1991, was to be levied on the amount of fixed capital investment incurred by indigenous enterprises. The standard rate was 15 per cent.[16]

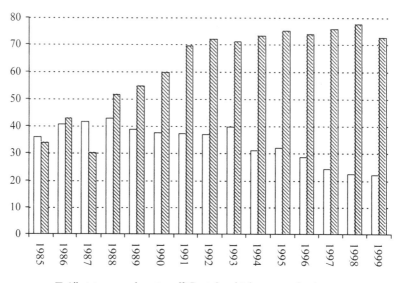

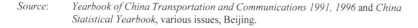

□ All state-owned sectors ▨ Postal and telecommunications sector

Source: *Yearbook of China Transportation and Communications 1991, 1996* and *China Statistical Yearbook*, various issues, Beijing.

Figure 2.4   Weight of technical upgrading and transformation investment in total fixed capital investment (1985–1999)

For projects that are of an inefficient scale, employing outmoded technologies, or making products already in excess supply, the state policy was to strictly control their development and therefore the highest rate of 30 per cent was applied.[17] For projects encouraged by the state but constrained by energy supply and transportation facilities, the low 5 per cent tax rate applied. The most favourable zero-tax rate applied to those projects 'urgently needed by the state'. All fixed capital investment in the postal and telecom sector enjoyed the zero-rate treatment. Other zero-rate projects included fixed capital investment in agriculture and water conservancy, energy, transportation, key raw materials, geological prospecting, certain medical research, certain electronic and machinery investment, pollution control, urban public utilities, some storage facilities and so on. This preferential investment policy was only phased out after 1998 when Beijing sought to boost the domestic demand by fiscal pump priming.

2.5   CAPITAL FORMATION

Backed by strong state support, capital accumulation in the telecom sector snowballed over the past two decades. A combination of strong internal incentives for network expansion, state policy support and the opening of multiple channels for capital financing led to a steep growth of fixed capital investment in the telecom infrastructure. As shown in Figure 2.5, the share of the telecom sector in China's total fixed capital investment started to rise sharply in the late 1980s and continued the trend throughout the 1990s. It rose from half a per cent in the first half of the 1980s to over 4 per cent after 1994, reaching above 7 per cent in recent years. Its total amount rose by 14 times from 1985 to 2000.

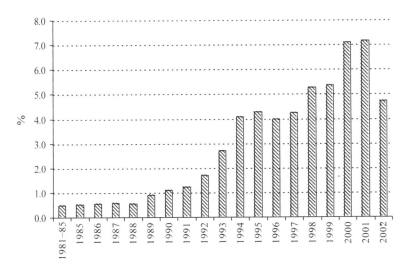

Source: *Yearbook of China Transportation and Communications* and *China Statistical Yearbook*, various issues. Ministry of Information Industry website, http://www.mii.gov.cn/.

Figure 2.5   Telecom sector's share in China's total fixed capital investment (1981–2002)

According to the MPT, during the first half of the 1990s, the investment in telecom infrastructure was mainly financed through three sources. One was the installation fee collected from the users, which accounted for 40 per cent of the capital. The second came from domestic and foreign government loans, accounting for about 30 per cent of the total capital. The remaining 30 per cent arose from PTE's profits and capital depreciation.[18]

In 1980, the State Council adopted a policy of developing local (intra-city) telephone service with local (intra-city) telephone revenues. From then on, local PTEs gained full control over the local (intra-city) telephone service revenues. In addition, local PTEs were authorized to charge phone subscribers expensive installation fees, which became an important source of capital accumulation. The practice started in 1980 to meet the fast-growing demand and to overcome fund shortage in telecom infrastructure investment. The State Council authorized PTAs to collect installation fees ranging between RMB 1,000 to RMB 2,000 per terminal for commercial telephone lines and between RMB 300 to RMB 500 for residential users.[19] In 1990, the MPT adjusted its guidelines for telephone installation fees. The installation fee charges were then based on line connection costs. Meanwhile, the decision making regarding installation charges was decentralized to the local level. In the early 1990s, the installation charges varied from around RMB 2,000 to more than RMB 5,000 per line (Liu, 1992). In comparison, in 1990, the average annual wage and per capita GDP were only RMB 2,140 and RMB 1,622, respectively. These figures indicate that, if an average worker wanted to subscribe a telephone line, he had to work 1–2.5 years just to pay the installation charge. Relative to per capita income, such an installation charge was the highest in the world.

Wu Jichuan, the Minister of the MPT, estimated that in 1995 the revenue from installation fees collected from installing 15 million telephone terminals amounted to RMB 45 billion. This revenue accounted for about half of the annual investment capital in 1995.[20]

As discussed above, the accounting rules to determine a PTE's revenue and wage fund provided strong incentives to business expansion. Meanwhile, the accounting rules for business expenses in the MPT system allowed the PTE managers to aggressively invest in network expansion. The system of 'special funding accounts' practised before 1993 separated the PTEs' capital expense and operation expense with rigid specification of fund uses according to fund sources. Under this system, once capital was raised, the marginal opportunity cost of facility investment appeared to be zero or external to the PTEs. As long as the PTEs and PTBs could raise capital from the state, banks or users, the investment in telecom network capacity would be risk-free to the managers. This arrangement drove the PTEs and PTBs to raise as much capital as possible to invest in infrastructure expansion.

The shortcomings of the incentive structure were obvious. It provided very little incentive for PTEs to economize operation and investment expenses. Nor did it give enough stimuli for firms to improve service quality and to introduce new service products. Notwithstanding that, the incentive structure did give a big push to the expansion of telecom network through infrastructure investment, which had also been supported by a series of external incentives.

Starting in the late 1980s, the intra-provincial telecom projects became financed mainly by local PTAs, which raised and collected funds from institutions or individuals. According to the '16-character policy' of 1988, the State Council explicitly defined the division of responsibilities between the ministry and the local government. The MPT should invest in equipment and machinery while the local government should invest in cable and line construction (Gao, 1991). Telecom infrastructure development was incorporated into provincial development plans. Most provincial legislature bodies had passed laws and regulations to define the division of responsibilities between the MPT and the local governments.[21]

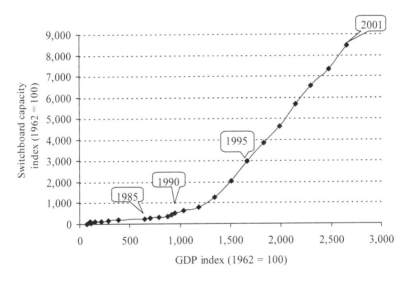

Source: *China Statistical Yearbook* and *Yearbook of China's Transportation and Communications*, various issues, Beijing.

Figure 2.6 *GDP index versus switchboard capacity index (1952–2001)*

The multi-investor feature of joint venture projects called for better-defined property rights. In July 1993, all PTEs established the capital account system to replace the earlier system of 'special funding accounts'. The reform ensured that the PTE could raise capital in various ways and manage the invested capital as a legal person.[22] This reform also allowed the PTEs greater autonomy to manage infrastructure development. In 1994, the MPT specified two measures to reward non-MPT investors in trial projects of joint ventures.

One is fixed-rate remuneration and the other is dividend distribution.[23] These reward arrangements paved the way for the corporatization of the PTEs in more recent years.

In the decade after 1984, fast capital accumulation in the telecom sector accelerated switchboard capacity growth by leaps and bounds. As shown in Figure 2.6, the accumulated growth of switchboard capacity overtook that of GDP in 1994 for the first time after 1962. The growth of switchboard capacity increased 14.5 times in the 1990s, dwarfing its accumulated growth in the previous decades.

Backed by strong state support and preferential policies, the MPT-controlled business empire once enjoyed the status of a privileged monopoly in its heyday until the late 1990s. With increasing participation of non-MPT investors in infrastructure construction and rising demand for better and more telecom services, the call for competition became increasingly compelling in the 1990s and eventually made its way to the government's agenda. China's telecom market has since then entered an age of competition.

Summary

The hyper growth of China's telecom industry in the last two decades was mainly driven by several important forces. On the demand side, the fast-growing economy and rising income fuelled the hungry demand for telecom services. On the supply side, reforms in the state-owned telecom industry created strong incentives for business expansion. Organizational restructure made it more effective for a nationwide network expansion plan to be implemented. A series of preferential policies made it easier for the state-owned telecom industry to raise funds and exercise its market power. Favourable tax rates and a huge amount of state capital injection also helped the industry to take off.

NOTES

1. According to official statistics, China's GDP slumped over 23 per cent in 1960–62. The recession concurred with the great famine of 1959–61, which caused 20–30 million excess deaths. See Johnson (1998) for more discussions on the famine.
2. Yearbook of China Transportation and Communications 1986, p. 243.
3. The MPT, 'Proposal to Reform Postal and Telecommunications Administration System (April 1979)', in *Yearbook of China Transportation and Communications 1986*, p. 342.

4.   In Chinese: 'zheng qi fen kai, you dian fen ying, qiye hesuan, zi ji ying kui' (Gao, 1991).

5.   The accounting system for long-distance service commenced in 1985 with a simple record of the firm's long-distance revenue and operation costs. Since a telecom service is a two-way exchange, the increase of real business revenue at one location may not necessarily reflect the growth of service quantity provided by the firm at that location. Therefore the system was adjusted and improved in 1988 on a concept of network revenue (Lu, 1994).

6.   Yearbook of China Transportation and Communications 1996, p. 234.

7.   State Council, 'Instruction to the Postal and Telecommunications Management (12 October 1984)', in *Yearbook of China Transportation and Communications 1986*, p. 243.

8.   An MPT source disclosed that in 1993 the profit margin on local service was only 2–3 per cent, while the margin on long-distance calls was 25 per cent and on international calls, 75 per cent (Mueller and Tan, 1997, p. 41).

9.   Yearbook of China Transportation and Communications 1990, pp. 270–271.

10.   The MPT, 'Measures to Link PTA Wage Funds to Revenues (August 1988)', in *Yearbook of China Transportation and Communications 1989*, pp. 614–615.

11.   In Chinese: 'tong chou guihua, tiao kuai jiehe, fen ceng fu ze, lianhe jianshe'.

12.   State Council, 'Instruction to the Postal and Telecommunications Management (12 October 1984)', *Yearbook of China Transportation and Communications 1986*, p. 243.

13.   Yearbook of China Transportation and Communications 1990, p. 271.

14.   The detailed depreciation scale is: 5–7 years for telecom equipment, 6–8 years for power equipment, 10–15 years for communications cables, 30–40 years for buildings (*Yearbook of China Transportation and Communications 1994*, p. 235).

15.   Wu Jichuan's interview, *Yazhou Zhoukan* (The International Chinese News Weekly), 19 May 1996, p. 58.

16.   State Council, 'The Provisional Regulation on the PRC's Direction-adjustment Tax on Fixed Capital Investment' (16 April 1991), Zhang and Wu (1994), pp. 584–605.

17.   Based on the same principle, the state has also promulgated a list of forbidden projects.

18.   *Lianhe Zaobao* (*United Mornings*, Singapore), 8 April 1994, p. 23.

19. Directive issued by Ministry of Finance, the MPT and State Bureau of Price On Urban Telephone Installation Fees (June 1980), in *Yearbook of China Transportation and Communications 1986*, pp. 344–345.
20. Wu Jichuan's interview, *Yazhou Zhoukan* (The International Chinese News Weekly), 19 May 1996, p. 58.
21. Yearbook of China Transportation and Communications 1992, p. 181.
22. Yearbook of China Transportation and Communications 1994, p. 235.
23. The MPT, 'Instruction on Trial Joint Venture Projects to Speed Up Telecommunications Development (September 1994)', in Y*earbook of China Transportation and Communications 1995*, p. 513.

3. Opening of a mega market

Before the mid-1980s, in most countries, the telecommunications (telecom) market was the oyster of either a state-owned postal, telephone and telegraph (PTT) monopoly or a regulated private monopoly like the US AT&T-Bell group before its divestiture. China's telecom sector used to be no exception but for its being part of the overall centrally planned economy, with or without a prioritized status. Since the early 1980s, the world's telecom sector has gone through revamps towards market openness and competition. In China, backed by state support, the privileged Ministry of Post and Telecommunications (MPT) regime made strides in building up the nation's telecom·infrastructure from the mid-1980s to the 1990s. No sooner had the regime managed to cash in its achievement than the clamour of competition broke into its oyster.

3.1   A COMPETITIVE EQUIPMENT MARKET

Competition first arrived in China's telecom equipment market in 1988 when the MPT system underwent a revamp amid a major state-owned enterprise reform initiative taking place nationwide. In this revamp, the MPT granted its national manufacturing, construction and purchasing departments the status of separate legal entities or greater independence in financial accounting and human resource management. Meanwhile the MPT set up the Directorate General of Telecommunications (DGT), which was later corporatized as China Telecom in 1995. In the same vein, all province-level post and telecom administrations (PTAs) were instructed in 1989 to set up their own telecom regulatory bodies and to reform their business branches into separate spin-offs.

   The reform in 1988 not only separated telecom equipment manufacturing from telecom service provision in the MPT regime but also shifted more decision-making authorities regarding procurement, operations, network development and financing from the MPT headquarters to the municipal and county post and telecom enterprises (PTEs). In 1989, the MPT took an important step towards a competitive equipment manufacturing market by issuing the terminal equipment licensing scheme.[1] This scheme largely deregulated the terminal equipment market to allow customers of the network to make their own choices over equipment purchase. As a result, the PTEs were free to choose among competing domestic and even foreign equipment suppliers. The purchasing and production of network equipment became increasingly competitive in the domestic market.

Low trade barriers for telecom equipment imports also contributed to promoting competitiveness of the market. Since the early 1980s, to encourage telecom investment, the government has granted preferential tariff treatment to the import of telecom equipment. In 1985, for instance, the import tariff rate on automatic exchanges and telefax equipment was cut from 12.5 per cent to 9 per cent.[2] For projects involving foreign investment, import tariffs were usually exempt. In comparison, China's average tariff rate was 39.9 per cent before 1994 and this was reduced to 23 per cent by 1996.

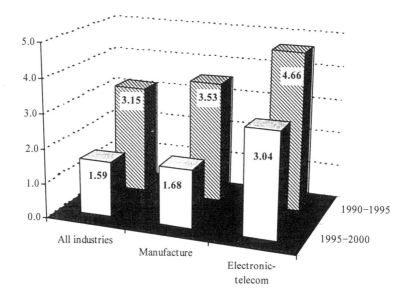

Source: *China Statistical Yearbook 1990, 1995, 2000.*

Figure 3.1   Sales revenue increase in the 1990s (unit: times)

The manufacturing of telecom equipment has also been open for foreign direct investment. In this field, Bell Shanghai and Shenda Telecom (in Shenzhen) are the two earliest manufacturing joint ventures in China (Zhou, 1991). The 1994 reform in foreign exchange management made Chinese currency virtually convertible for current account transactions and greatly reduced the foreign exchange risk in using foreign capital. By the late 1990s, virtually all internationally branded mobile telephone manufacturers, including Motorola, Siemens and Nokia, had set up their productions lines in China. The mobile telecom equipment output increased 2.6 times from 121.3 thousand units in 1995 to 320.3 units in 1999.[3]

Throughout the 1990s, the electronic and telecom sub-industry demonstrated the fastest growth of sales revenue in the manufacturing industry (Figure 3.1). Besides strong market demand, a favourable factor behind the boom of the telecom equipment manufacturing was state policies. Since the late 1980s, the major cross-industry difference in tax burden has been embedded in sales-related taxes, such as tax on city maintenance and construction, consumption tax, resource tax and extra levies for education and community development, and so on. Table 3.1 illustrates sectoral differences in sales-related tax burdens by displaying the effective sales-related tax rates on revenues. In all the three snapshot years (1990, 1995 and 2000), producers of electronic and telecom equipment enjoyed the lowest effective rate among all industries.

Table 3.1   *Effective rate of sales-related taxes for industrial enterprises by sector*

	1990	1995	2000
Heavy industry	7.59	6.48	5.86
Of which: manufacturing	5.13	4.79	4.20
• Special purpose equipment	5.44	4.55	4.21
• Electronic and telecom equipment	3.77	2.81	2.61
• Instruments, meters, cultural and official machinery	5.69	4.62	3.13
National total	8.25	6.45	6.08

Note: Sales-related tax is the difference between sales profit and total profit. The effective rate of sales-related tax is calculated by dividing the difference by the sales revenue.

Source: *China Statistical Yearbook 1990, 1995, 2000.*

3.2   EMERGING COMPETITION IN THE SERVICE MARKET

The year 1992 was a turning point in China's economic development and market-oriented reform. In spring that year, Deng Xiaoping, China's late paramount leader, who had officially retired, made a tour to several cities in South China during which he called on the new generation of leaders to speed up economic reform and make the economy more open to the world. Answering Deng's call, the Chinese Communist Party's 14th National Assembly (held in October 1992) formally adopted 'a socialist market economy with Chinese characteristics' as the goal model of reform. This marked the beginning of a series of centrally initiated reforms to usher in a modern market economy for China. The reform package implemented in 1994–95 covered the fiscal taxation system, money and banking, and foreign exchange management. The central and the local governments made concerted efforts to attract foreign direct investment by offering low-priced land, quality infrastructure, tax concessions and improved public services. China became the world's second largest host country for foreign capital inflow, next only to the US, in 1993 and remained so through the 1990s. During the decade, China sucked in about half of all foreign direct investment that went to the developing economies. Thanks to these reforms, China's gross domestic product (GDP) grew at an annual rate of 11.9 per cent and its investment at 14.1 per cent during 1990–97, much higher than the rates for low- and middle-income economies in the same period (2.8 per cent and 7.2 per cent respectively).[4]

Tussles for Power

In this backdrop of market-oriented reform, the centrally planned hierarchy of the MPT monopoly in the public telecom service market and network development was inevitably challenged. Despite the MPT's spectacular success in building up the telecom infrastructure, its mandate over the industry started to shake.

It is interesting to note that, even in the era of central economic planning, the telecom service market was for years under a fragmented administrative structure. As shown in Chapter 2, from 1973 to 1979, the governments at the levels of province, municipality and prefecture had the actual control over the planning of postal and telecom business in their domains. The MPT did not have exclusive power in regulating the whole telecom sector.

Throughout the 1980s, the MPT made important achievements in rebuilding its centralized control over the public telecom sector. It also managed to assume a greater role in overseeing the whole telecom industry. This was reflected in the State Council's '16-character policy' of 1988 for telecom development, which clearly stated that 'overall planning of industrial development should be unified under the MPT'. However, the same document also stated that the 'ministerial administration should be coordinated with regional authorities', which continued to hold big stakes in local network assets.

On the other hand, over years, several government ministerial branches developed a number of non-public/dedicated communication networks (vis-à-vis the MPT-managed public network) for their own interior uses. These included the networks under Ministry of Railways, Ministry of Electrical Power, China Academy of Science and State Education Commission, as well as the People's Liberation Army (PLA). In some regions, the capacity of some of these networks was no inferior to the capacity of the MPT-managed public network (He, 1994). The jurisdiction of these ministerial branches over these 'dedicated' telecom systems went beyond the MPT's domain.

The overall coordination of telecom policies in this fragmented administrative system was realized through the State Council, which was involved in regulatory routine at the highest level. Among ministries under the State Council, the MPT was the only ministry that combined the functions of policy/regulation and public telecom service provision under its umbrella. Its monopoly over the public service market and its growing clout to oversee 'overall planning of industrial development' increasingly conflicted with the interests of other ministerial branches, particularly when huge market potentials for telecom services emerged in the early 1990s. As pointed out by Tan (1994):

> Big private [non-public] operators and manufacturing ministries often confront the MPT in the arenas of policy and regulation. ... [T]hey have the same, or even stronger, levels of representation in the State Council, ... Large users and local governments also tend to favour a more liberal policy towards public service and they are dissatisfied with the MPT's monopoly. At the equipment end, Ministry of Electronic Industry (MEI) and some user ministries are the traditional competitors (to the MPT) ... (Tan, 1994)

Triggering the Fall of a Giant

The first crack in the MPT monopoly regime cropped up in the non-basic telecom service segments. In 1993, the State Council formally deregulated the paging service market and the VSAT communications by authorizing the MPT to license these service suppliers.[5] By the end of 1995, the MPT had licensed 2,136 paging service suppliers and 68 inter-provincial VSAT communications service providers.[6] In the paging market, the MPT-affiliated enterprises as a whole continued to be a leading player, which later formed Guoxin Paging Limited when the business was split in 1998 from China Telecom. In the satellite communications market, the MPT-affiliated China Satellite Telecom Group Corp (ChinaSat, founded in 1985) maintained a lead throughout the 1990s, followed by the Sino Satellite Communications, a non-MPT consortium formed by several ministries in 1994, and China Orient, another player with the MPT as the holding shareholder (Gao and Lyytinen, 2000).

Jitong Communications Company Limited (Beijing) was the first major value-added network (VAN) operator that entered the market in June 1993. Set up by the State Economic and Trade Commission, Jitong's shareholders came from 30 state-owned enterprises and research institutes in Beijing, Guangzhou, Shanghai and Shenzhen. Its primary functions include setting up joint ventures with overseas companies in communications research and product development, building local trunk radio, paging and cellular networks, and developing a nationwide backbone linking the networks belonging to government ministries, universities, and research and state-owned organizations (Ure, 1994). It was also supposed to offer VAN services to government departments and the private sector.

A major breakthrough took place when in December 1993 the State Council decided to award a basic telecom licence to China United Telecommunications Corporation (or Unicom).[7] China Unicom was set up by three powerful ministries, namely Ministry of Electronic Industries, the Ministry of Railways, the Ministry of Electric Power and 13 major state-owned companies. The carrier intended to compete with the MPT in the long-distance and international services market.

The birth of China Unicom was a result of high-level 'lobbying' by a political coalition formed by the three powerful ministries (He, 1994; Tan, 1994). A footnote to this coalition's power base is that Jiang Zemin, the Communist Party's Secretary General (1989–2002), used to be the Minister of Electronic Industries in the early 1980s. Li Peng, the Premier until 1998, also served as Minister of Electric Power in his earlier career. The emergence of China Unicom and other new players in the industry was 'a product more of political power than of market economy. The competition arising from it was conducted in the absence of a developed legal framework' (Jing, 1999).

The State Council adopted the proposal to issue the licence to China Unicom while reaffirming the leading role of the MPT in the sector and its functions of network supervision and regulation. As noted by Mueller and Tan (1997), the MPT's primary role in the telecom sector was severely circumvented since the new players like China Unicom had a power base outside the MPT that placed them 'almost at the same level in deliberations regarding the sector's future structure'. To resolve the inevitable disagreements among the ministerial stakeholders, in 1994 the State Council created a national Joint Conference on State Economic Informatization (JCSEI), chaired by Vice-Premier Zou Jiahua.

Both Unicom and Jitong were shareholder-based but largely state-owned and state-controlled. After that, China Telecom, the former MPT-controlled monopoly, had gradually lost its grip over the nation's huge public telecom market and eventually succumbed to its own fate of divestiture. A number of political-economic factors were behind these developments.

Changes in Mindset

In correspondence to the formation of JCSEI, the State Council announced in 1994 the 'eight policies of telecommunications development',[8] which outlined China's renewed strategies of developing the sector:

1. Giving priority and policy support to the telecom sector.
2. Unified central planning of network and service development.
3. Focusing on the construction of a unified nationwide public network.
4. Licensing value-added and mobile telecom services; deregulating the equipment manufacturing market; conducting open tender for network projects.
5. Independent accounting and hierarchical administration for the PTEs; linking employee rewards to enterprise performance.
6. Supporting the PTEs to raise capital from various ways and collect installation fees.
7. Promoting network modernization and human resource development.
8. Importing foreign equipment and technology and utilizing foreign fund sources.

These policies reflect a gradualist and cautious approach to market opening. It reflected the changes in the mindset of China's central planners for telecom development as well as a compromise of interests between the MPT and its challengers.

From the 1980s to the 1990s, rapid technological progress in telecom technology was moving the industry in many countries towards a more competitive and deregulated regime. Telecom used to be a classical case of an industry with 'natural monopoly' features. Economic efficiency brought about by economies of scale created formidable entry barriers for any firms intending to compete against the incumbent monopoly. Cross-subsidization between profitable and unprofitable segments of the market was viewed as a necessary 'sin' with the provision of 'universal service' to the public. New communications technology has made such an industrial structure unsustainable and obsolete. Since the early 1980s, in developed countries like the US, Britain and Australia, competition introduced by the regulatory revamp in the telecom market has greatly boosted the sector's growth and has improved customer service.[9]

In China, this global trend lent strong support to the challengers of the MPT monopoly. To the top Chinese leaders, the application of information technology (IT) is indispensable for modernising the economy and reviving science, technology and education. Aware of the rationale behind the global trend of a market opening in the telecom industry, the Chinese leaders could not afford to allow China's IT industry to be constrained by inefficiency, poor service and high prices, which were associated with the nature of a state monopoly.

In the late 1980s and early 1990s, the customer base for a telephone service was quickly privatized. A telephone service was no longer only an administrative tool of the state, but a private good for business operation and household consumption. In 1991, residential phones accounted for more than one-third of the total telephones in more than ten provinces and municipals (Hong and Qian, 1992). In 1995, more than 80 per cent of the increased telephone exchange capacity was for residential use.[10] With a fast increasing customer base, the public cries for better services, more options and lower tariff rates grew louder.

However, the central planning mindset nurtured what Mueller and Tan (1997) called a 'technocratic approach' to IT development. This approach sees technology as a paramount factor in economic development, as opposed to the 'market-oriented approach', which sees market forces as the means to economic development. The Chinese leaders with technocratic views saw the application of IT as a crucial factor in attempting to bring the economy under some kind of systematic central control. They also viewed information networks as the equivalent of price signals, profit incentives and legal structures that promote coordination in a market economy. These views prompted them to maintain central control over telecom network building while introducing competition in a prudent and gradualist manner.

Within the MPT, a representative view towards competition and monopoly in the industry is based on the thesis of a 'post-telephony era'. According to this thesis, telecom development must go through two stages. The first is the telephony era, during which infrastructure-building raises teledensity to meet the need of universal service for basic telephony. The second is the post-telephony era, featured by pluralized and more advanced communications services, which add value to the public network built in the first stage. In the first era, the industry has the features of a natural monopoly with strong economies of scale and therefore would be best managed in a centrally planned monopoly system. A competitive market would be efficiency-enhancing and conducive to technological progress only in the post-telephony era. Therefore, in the case of China, the rapid build-up of telecom infrastructure could only be carried out under a state-planned, monopolist regime, especially during the industry's takeoff period. With the basic public network in place, China quickly entered a transitional period between the two eras in the mid-1990s. In this period, state monopoly and central planning were still better able to raise teledensity and provide basic telephony to the population; as for the markets for plural and advanced services, it was better that they be made open to competition gradually (Jing, 1999).

3.3   TOWARDS GUIDED COMPETITION

The birth of Unicom and Jitong and the institutional change at the top decision-making authority, however, failed to create effective competition in the sector. The original purpose to license China Unicom was to let the new company unite the domestic non-public networks and use their capacity to compete with China Telecom, the dominant carrier transformed from the former monopolistic DGT of the MPT. However, it soon became clear that China Unicom was not able to fulfil the expectation largely due to its lack of expertise in telecom management and political clout to 'unite' different stakeholders.

Meanwhile, China Telecom was still directly under the MPT's control in the interim process of being corporatized. It was widely believed that the MPT was not an impartial referee but intervened on behalf of its favourites in the game. When Unicom was set up in 1994, Wu Jichuan, the MPT minister, was reportedly overheard saying that he wanted 'not only to strangle Unicom, but to bury it deep'. [11] It was therefore an unlevel playing field between the MEI-backed Unicom and the MPT-backed China Telecom. Thus in the first four years after the launch of Unicom, Unicom mainly focused itself on the mobile communications market, capturing only 3.5 per cent of the market share, compared to China Telecom's 96.5 per cent share (Jing, 1999).

Birth of a Regulatory Authority

The MPT was itself, however, a lame-duck regulator. It was not powerful enough to intervene effectively in other ministries' domains and had to turn to the State Council for resolving its conflicts with Unicom and its backing ministries from time to time (Gao and Lyytinen, 2000). At the super-ministerial level, the temporary 'task force' nature of the JCSEI prevented it from performing the role of an effective regulatory authority. In 1996 it was soon replaced by the National Information Infrastructure Steering Committee (NIISC), which was charged with responsibilities for the formulation and implementation of plans, policies and regulations in the information industry. The committee was still chaired by Vice Premier Zou, with ministers of MPT, MEI, the State Planning Commission (SPC), the State Science and Technology Commission (SSTC) and the People's Bank as the committee's deputy directors (Tan, 1999). The NIISC, however, was still an interim task force for inter-ministry coordination and negotiation, lacking the legislative status, financial means and administrative power to effectively enforce regulations.

Without a legal framework for regulation, the policy coordination carried out by the State Council was featured by ad hoc administrative intervention or arbitrated negotiations. As pointed out by Gao and Lyytinen (2000), the regime:

worked satisfactorily during the monopoly period. The public telecom was mainly handled by the MPT that had its own centralized administrative system. This enabled the MPT to harmonize policies within its domain. But as new services appeared and their markets opened from the late 1980s, this fragmented regime became inefficient.

Table 3.2   The eight ministries and commissions formed by the restructure of the State Council in 1998

Ministries and commissions before the restructure	Ministries and commissions after the restructure
State Planning Commission	State Development and Planning Commission
State Science and Technology Commission	Ministry of Science and Technology
• Ministry of Geology and Mineral Resources • State Land Administration • State Maritime Bureau • State Survey Bureau	Ministry of Land and Resources
State Education Commission	Ministry of Education
• Commission of Science, Technology, and Industry for National Defence • Department of National Defence of the State Planning Council • Governmental functions of Military Industry Companies	State Science, Technology and Industry Commission for National Defence
• Ministry of Labour • Social Security Department of Ministry of Personnel • Social Security Department of Ministry of Civil Affairs • Insurance Department of Ministry of Public Health	Ministry of Labour and Social Security

• Ministry of Electrical Industry • Ministry of Post and Communications • Network Department of Ministry of Radio, Film and Television	Ministry of Information Industry
• State Economic and Trade Commission • Ministry of Power • Ministry of Coal Industry • Ministry of Metallurgical Industry • Ministry of Machine-building • Ministry of Chemical Industry • Ministry of Internal Trade • Textile Industry Council • General Company of Petroleum and Gas • General Company of Chemical Industry	State Economic and Trade Commission

Note: Total number of ministries and commissions under the State Council was reduced from 40 to 29 at the 9th National People's Congress.

Source: Li (1998), pp. 25–27.

After a few years of tussle for power, the Ministry of Information Industry (MII) was created at the 9th National People's Congress (NPC) convened in March 1998. This occurred among the major reforms of the ministerial structure in the State Council. With these reforms, China abandoned the Soviet-type ministerial structure based on industrial-sectoral divisions. Total number of ministries and commissions under the State Council was reduced from 40 to 29 in this restructure (Table 3.2).

The ministries in this streamlined administrative structure function more like regulatory authorities or public service providers rather than state-owned industrial planners or managers. Intended to be an independent regulatory entity, the MII was formed through the merger of the former MPT, the former MEI and the Network Department of the former Ministry of Radio, Film and Television. This was a marriage between odd partners since the MPT and MEI had been rivals all these years.

In addition, the new ministry took over information and network administration, handled previously by the former JCSEI/NIISC and the former State Council's Commission on Radio Frequencies, the former Ministry of

Radio, Film and Television (MRFT), China Corporation of Aerospace Industry and China Corporation of Aviation Industry. Meanwhile, the former MRFT, which previously regulated the television industry, was downgraded to a sub-ministerial body under the State Council and became State Administration of Radio, Film and Television (SARFT), which is responsible for the regulation and operation of the CATV networks. In this restructure, the crucial personnel appointment was placing Wu Jichuan, the minister of the disbanding MPT, at the helm of the new ministry.

The MII-guided Competition

A major objective of this reform was to fulfil the separation of the regulatory and commercial functions in the info-communications sector so that competition can be developed under the supervision of a single and supposedly impartial regulatory authority, the MII. After this restructuring of the ministerial system, at least at the ministerial level, the MII forms a more coherent regulatory regime. With the mandate to restructure the telecom sector, the MII launched a new round of reforms to introduce guided competition into the industry.

The first job the MII accomplished was the successful separation of the former MPT's postal and telecom businesses. By early 1999, almost all assets and employees of the former PTEs under the MPT had been reallocated to the two separate business entities, China Post and China Telecom. After separation from the postal business, China Telecom had about RMB 600 billion worth of assets.[12] Prior to the complete corporatization of China Telecom, it launched 144 million IPO shares in the Hong Kong stock market in October 1997. The company was formed from several provincial GSM networks, with China Telecom holding 51 per cent of shares and other rations of shares floating on the Hong Kong stock market.

The next task for MII was to divest the former telecom monopoly into smaller entities so that effective competition could prevail. At first, some scholars in Beijing proposed a 'horizontal divestiture' of China Telecom into seven regional 'baby CTs' following the US model of the AT&T divestiture in 1983. With fierce opposition from the MII, the proposal was shot down after an official delegation that visited the US to investigate the background of AT&T divestiture reported that mergers, rather than divestiture, had become the trend in the industry. The delegation also reported that even officials of the US Federal Communications Commission (FCC) did not consider the AT&T divestiture model appropriate for China. After that, the MII won State Council approval for its 'vertical divestiture' plan. Based on this plan, the MII started in December 1999 to divest China Telecom into four separate companies serving different functions, namely, fixed-line, mobile, paging and satellite operations.

In fact, before its formal divestiture, China Telecom had already been operating under the framework of four business lines in 1999 (Wu, 2000). These were the China Telecom Group Corporation (with an asset value of about RMB 400 billion), the China Mobile Telecom Group Corporation (with an asset value of RMB 180 billion), the Guoxin Paging Telecom Group Corporation (with an asset value of RMB 13 billion) and the China Satellite Telecom Group Corporation (with an asset value less than RMB 1 billion).[13]

After China Telecom's vertical divestiture, in May 2000, the MII arranged for China Mobile Communications (Group) Corporation to become the new owner of China Telecom (Hong Kong) Company by acquiring at no cost China Telecom Group's stake in China Telecom (HK). Under the new name 'China Mobile (HK) Company', the giant-listed company in Hong Kong's stock market started preparations to purchase seven of the mainland's biggest provincial and municipal mobile-phone networks from its state-owned parent, China Mobile Communications Corporation. The regions covered were Beijing, Tianjin, Shanghai, Liaoning, Hebei, Shandong and Guangxi.[14] This acquisition was backed by Vodafone, who agreed in October 2000 to invest US$ 2.5 billion to help fund the US$ 34 billion deal. With this investment, Vodafone would gain a 2.6 per cent stake in China Mobile's current US$ 96 billion market value.[15]

As for China Unicom, rather than attempting to 'strangle' and 'bury deep' this four-year-old carrier, the MII led by Wu Jichuan worked hard to position China Unicom as an effective competitor to China Telecom and China Mobile. The following series of measures were taken to beef up Unicom:

- The first step taken by the MII was to make itself the largest stakeholder of China Unicom by transferring the entire assets of China Telecom's code division multiple access (CDMA) Great Wall Network and Guoxin Paging Company paging branch to Unicom in spring 1999.[16] The Great Wall Communications Limited was formed by the MPT and the PLA before 1998 to make effective use of frequencies owned by the army for developing the CDMA mobile telecom service. At the time when Guoxin (with assets valued at RMB 13 billion) was transferred to China Unicom, the latter had only assets worth RMB 2.3 billion (Gao and Lyytinen, 2000).

- The MII then moved to reshuffle the management of China Unicom by replacing its executives with experienced ones from China Telecom. The staff exchange and asset transfer are said to have contributed to an improved business relationship between the two rival carriers.[17]

- The MII allowed China Unicom to expand into mobile and Internet telephony. In particular, China Mobile was allowed to retain only the business of global system for mobile communications (GSM) and the analogue total access communications system (TACS) network. The whole CDMA market was reserved for Unicom (Li, 2000). In addition, for GSM services, China Unicom was given the privilege to compete by giving 10 per cent discounts on prices offered by China Mobile.

- China Unicom also received a boost in its efforts to compete against China Telecom when it obtained the MII's approval to enter the domestic and international long-distance call market in March 2000, thus effectively breaking the China Telecom monopoly in this lucrative market.[18]

- Last but not least, China Unicom got the MII's blessing to launch an initial public offering (IPO) to raise equity funds. It went 'public' by launching IPO in the Hong Kong and New York stock exchanges in June 2000 with a plan to raise at least US$ 1 billion, but ended up with a listed market value close to US$ 5 billion.[19] In March 2000, backed by the MII, China Unicom succeeded in procuring loans of RMB 10 billion and RMB 1.6 billion from the China Development Bank and the Bank of China, respectively, to finance its construction of mobile and digital communication networks.[20]

In January 2000, China Unicom signed an interconnection agreement with China Telecom. Under the agreement, China Unicom's long-distance networks in 25 coastal cities would be connected to China Telecom's fixed-line networks, while the latter would obtain 8 per cent of China Unicom's revenue from long-distance calls.[21] China Unicom subsequently unveiled detailed plans to capture more than 30 per cent of the mainland's fast-growing mobile phone and Internet-related services markets in the next five years. It plans to boost the capacity of its CDMA mobile-phone network to 60 million lines by 2005, aiming to attract 45 million subscribers, with the network covering most of the country. It believes that the capacity of its global system for mobile communications (GSM) network will by then reach 15 million lines and attract 13 million subscribers, with the network covering the prosperous eastern and middle parts of the country.[22]

3.4 ENTRY OF POWERFUL PLAYERS

As the MII exercised its mandate over a supposed-to-be controlled market opening process, more powerful new entrants were knocking at the door of the lucrative telecom market. The entry of these powerful players soon posed serious challenges to the MII's regulatory authority.

Railcom and Netcom

One entrant is China Railway Telecommunications and Information Corporation (China Railcom), which is owned by the Ministry of Railway (MOR), one of the powerful government departments that had long been vying for the telecom business. When Unicom was first set up to challenge the MPT's monopoly over the telecom sector, the MOR was one of the major stake owners of the company. Later, as the MII restructured Unicom by transferring assets and managerial personnel from the former China Telecom group in 1998–99, the MOR decided to set up its own telecom carrier, Railcom.

As early as June 1999, the MOR aired its decision to set up a public phone company based on its nationwide telecom system.[23] Claimed to be the country's largest exclusive network, the 120-year-old communication infrastructure had been in existence even before the postal system's network, with an estimated asset value of RMB 10 billion (US$ 1.21 billion).[24] It nevertheless took two-and-half years for Railcom to be licensed by the MII on 7 January 2001 to provide a basic fixed-line (local and long-distance) telecom service, Internet access and IP telephony. Being allowed to operate the fixed-line network and having operations in all but two of China's provinces, China Railcom was regarded as 'the first truly national competitor to China Telecom'.[25]

Compared to Railcom, China Netcom Corporation, launched in April 1999, had a much smaller initial physical asset but stronger political clout. With RMB 420 million (US$ 50.6 million) in start-up capital,[26] Netcom soon announced a grand plan to construct a broadband network and to provide a high-speed voice and data service in 15 cities, and to connect with 70 countries.[27] Two of the four partners of this joint venture set up by the Chinese Academy of Sciences, the Shanghai Municipal Government, SARFT and MOR, were long-time rivals of the MII. Notwithstanding that, Netcom was 'considered to be insulated from regulatory risk because it boasts Jiang Mianheng, the eldest son of President Jiang Zemin, was one of its directors'.[28] The new entrant very soon became the favoured company for foreign investors to seek partnerships with.

The company was thus able to raise in 2000 an estimated US$ 300 million in equity financing from a consortium of investors, which reportedly include three US companies (Dell Computer, Goldman Sachs and Rupert Murdoch's News Corporation) and three Hong Kong companies (Sun Hung Kai, Henderson Land and the Kerry Group). At the end of 2000, the telecom operator launched its Internet data services to almost 100,000 subscribers in 17 major cities (most of them along the eastern seaboard). The 9,600-km network comprised three sections (Beijing-Wuhan-Guangzhou, Beijing-Tianjin-Shanghai and Shanghai-Xiamen-Guangzhou). With financial backing by foreign capital and state banks as well as its unique political clout, Netcom planned to eventually develop its backbone network to cover 60–100 cities in later phases of development that might take at least 2–3 years to build. Total investment was likely to exceed US$ 2.5 billion.[29] In 2001, Netcom even started buying up broadband cable from local cable television companies, not shying away from its ambition to become a major provider of not only telecom services but also cable television.

The aggressive broadband network investment plans of these new entrants challenged the MII's unified national planning for network development. The ensuing regulatory battles eroded the MII's authority over the market opening process (see Chapter 4).

More Competitive Services

Along with the divestiture of China Telecom and the beefing-up of China Unicom, the telecom sector in the last few years has witnessed a series of reforms that featured market opening, tariff readjustment and the formulation and completion of telecom legislation. The expensive installation fees have been cut and finally eliminated. High rates for long-distance and international calls have been slashed. At the provincial level, however, the restructuring of the old PTA–PTB hierarchy had not been fulfilled by early 2000 (Wu, 2000).

Table 3.3   Market shares in the first half of 2000

	China Telecom	China Mobile	Unicom	Jitong	Netcom
Total telephone user base	68.1	25.8	6		
Long-distance optical cable	86.6		13.4		
Mobile phone subscription		81.2	18.8		
IP telephony	54.4		31.2	12.3	2.1

Source: Zhongguo Jingji Shibao (China Economic Times), 20 October 2000.

Since its inception, the MII has also been the agency authorised to review, approve and grant operation licences to Internet Service Providers (ISPs). In 1999, the MII and its provincial PTAs approved more than 300 ISPs, among which 53 were approved for nationwide services.[30] With the blessing of the MII, China Telecom launched a nationwide Internet protocol (IP) telephony trial in May 1999 in partnership with state-owned carriers Jitong Communications and China Unicom. In April 2000, after nearly a one-year trial period, the MII formally issued four IP telephony licences to China Telecom, China Unicom,

Jitong Communications and China Netcom.[31] Since then, competition has emerged in the long-distance call market.

The MII's work to divest China Telecom and beef up Unicom took immediate effect. In 1999, China Unicom had only 5 per cent of the mobile phone market but it was able to increase its share to 12 per cent after it received asset and personnel transfer from China Telecom in early 2000.[32] The launch of IP telephony and Unicom's entry into the international direct dial (IDD) call service in early 2000 marked the beginning of a more competitive market structure in the long-distance market. China's telecom sector thus entered an era of competition by the end of the 1990s (see Table 3.3).

After the launch of Railcom, the Chinese telecom market had a total of six major players (Table 3.4) in 2001. All six players engaged in backbone network development, which was closely overseen by the MII. The IP telephony and internet access markets became fairly competitive with all but one player (China Mobile) competing among themselves. The mobile telephone market became a duopoly shared between China Mobile and Unicom. As for the local fixed-line and long-distance market, despite the limited competition posed by Unicom and Railcom, the dominance of China Telecom was still overwhelming.

Table 3.4   Business scopes of six major carriers (2001)

	China Telecom	China Mobile	Unicom	Jitong	Netcom	Railcom
Local fixed line	Y		*Y**			*Y*
Long distance	Y		*Y*			*Y*
Backbone network	Y	Y	Y	Y	Y	Y
IP telephony	Y		Y	Y	Y	Y
Internet access	Y		Y	Y	Y	Y
Mobile telephony		Y	Y			

Note: Italic 'Y' refers to business presence with geographic restrictions or of little significance.

Summary

China opened its telecom equipment market much earlier than its telecom service market. With low tariff rates and foreign direct investment, the domestic equipment market became fairly competitive in the late 1980s. The emergence of domestic competition in the telecom service market during the 1990s was mainly caused by the combined effects of forced entry of powerful interests, a restructure of regulatory regime, and changes in the mindset of policy makers and regulators.

NOTES

1. Yearbook of China Transportation and Communications 1996, p. 232.
2. *Almanac of China's Foreign Economic Relations 1986*, Beijing: Foreign Trade and Economic Cooperation Press, p. 129.
3. China Statistical Yearbook 1996, 2000.
4. World Bank, *World Development Report 1998/99*, Table 11, pp. 210–211.
5. State Council, 'Approval of the MPT's Proposal to Enforce Regulation of Telecommunications Service Market (3 August 1993)', in *Yearbook of China Transportation and Communications 1994*, pp. 468–469.
6. Yearbook of China Transportation and Communications 1996, pp. 231–232.
7. The MPT, 'Approval of China United Telecom's Scope of Business (14 April 1994)', in *Yearbook of China Transportation and Communications 1995*, p. 512.
8. Yearbook of China Transportation and Communications 1995, p. 225.
9. *China Daily* (Hong Kong), 10 June 1999.
10. Wu Jichuan's interview, *Yazhou Zhoukan (The International Chinese News Weekly)*, 19 May 1996, pp. 57–58.
11. 'Chinese telecoms: into the crucible', *The Economist* (UK), 1 November 2001.
12. Interview with officials and scholars of the Shanghai Institute of P & T Economy, 20 June 1999.
13. Interview with officials and scholars of the Shanghai Institute of P & T Economy, 20 June 1999.
14. 'China Telecom (HK) Changes Name to China Mobile', *China Online News*, 22 May 2000, http://www.chinaonline.com.
15. 'Vodafone buys into China Mobile', *Straits Times* (Singapore), 5 October 2000.
16. *China Online News*, 4 May 1999, http://www.chinaonline.com.

17. Interview with officials and scholars of the Shanghai Institute of P & T Economy, 20 June 1999, 8 July 2000.
18. *South China Morning Post* (Hong Kong), 11 March 2000.
19. *South China Morning Post* (Hong Kong), 15 April 2000; Lin (2000); and *China Online News*, 21 June 2000.
20. *China Daily* (Hong Kong), 23 March 2000; *South China Morning Post* (Hong Kong), 1 April 2000.
21. *South China Morning Post* (Hong Kong), 21 March 2000.
22. *South China Morning Post* (Hong Kong), 15 December 1999.
23. 'Railways Ministry in China Ready to Become Full Service Telecommunications Provider', *China Online News,* 14 June 1999 http://www.chinaonline.com.
24. 'Railways Ministry in China Ready to Become Full Service Telecommunications Provider', *China Online News,* 14 June 1999 http://www.chinaonline.com.
25. *Business China* (London), 29 January 2001.
26. 'New telecom upstart, China Netcom, moves up launch to mid October', *China Online News*, 20 September 1999.
27. *South China Morning Post* (Hong Kong), 15 December 1999.
28. 'China's tangled broadband revolution', *Financial Times* (FT.com), 1 August 2001.
29. 'Netcom moves to offer Internet services', *China Online News*, 8 November 2000.
30. Xinhua News Agency, 16 February 2000, http://www.xinhua.org/chanjing.
31. MII's announcement on the opening of IP telephony market, 24 March 2000 (MII website news, 30 March 2000, http://www.mii.gov.cn.)
32. *China Daily* (Hong Kong), 10 June 1999; 23 March 2000.

4. Forming a regulatory framework

The Ministry of Information Industry's (MII) substitution for the Ministry of Post and Telecommunications (MPT) in the spring of 1998 ended the period of asymmetric regulation biased to China Telecom and the fragmented administrative regime in which the MPT played a lame-duck role, as observed by Gao and Lyytinen (2000). With the major rival ministries of the MPT being either merged into the new MII, downgraded to sub-ministerial entities, or taken over by other ministerial commissions, apparently there were no longer any serious threats to the MII's regulatory authority.

The unfolding of events since then, however, suggests that the formation of a consistent regulatory framework for China's telecom market has never been an easy task. In the first place, there was no Telecommunications Law to define the MII's regulatory authority and regulatory principles. Since its birth, the MII has had to fight for its regulatory authority. Thanks to various interest groups craving for the telecom market, the MII's plans and controls are frequently challenged and circumvented. The MII-centred regulatory regime turned out to be unstable.

4.1 IMPERFECT GUIDANCE

Introducing guided competition has been a priority on the MII's agenda. Since early 1999, the MII has openly promoted its development strategy for the telecom industry, which is summarized as 'breaking up the monopoly and introducing competition' (*pochu longduan, yinru jingzheng*). The strategy claims to rely on the market to improve telecom services and accelerate technological progress to prepare the sector for global competition.[1]

MII's Guiding Plan

With a closer look, the basic idea behind these MII-initiated reforms consists of the following points (Jing, 1999)[2]:

- Emphasizing unified planning and coordination in developing the basic network to avoid repeated building up of expensive networks;

- Opening the service business to fair competition;
- Allowing access to the backbone network, which is to be kept under unified investment and management;
- Imposing strict regulation on basic services while having looser regulation on value-added services;
- Strengthening the role of dominant state carriers when opening the market to more competition; and
- Continuing policies to favour telecom network development in rural and underdeveloped areas.

Of these points, the crucial ones are 'unified investment and management' for backbone network development and 'strengthening the role of dominant state carriers'. They reflect the MII's intention to maintain the dominance of the fixed network carrier, China Telecom, and keep its control over the access to backbone network resources. The vertical divestiture plan for the pre-1998 China Telecom fitted these policies and so did the MII's initiative to beef up Unicom. They all worked to ensure that the services provided by new carriers would simply complement China Telecom's basic services and not pose a direct threat to its dominance.

In the first two years after the inception of the MII, the vertical divestiture of China Telecom merely split the telecom market into several highly monopolistic segments and created only limited competition (Chapter 3, Table 3.3). The China Telecom-China Mobile business alliance continued to dominate the market for basic long-distance and mobile services. China Telecom still had about 99 per cent share of the fixed-line market. Its main competitor, China Unicom, had a basic service network in only three cities: Tianjin, Chongqing and Chengdu. As observed by Hsu (1999), the presence of these new carriers might not signify genuine deregulation and competition, since it was the MII, not market demand, which directed their moves. Meanwhile, the historical links between the MII and the major state-owned carriers cast doubts on the MII's capacity as an impartial regulator.

A New Round of Challenges

The MII-guided market opening process, however, was short-lived and very soon encountered a new round of challenges from other ministries and interest groups. The technological background of this new round of challenges is the development of broadband network in the 1990s, which has called into question, as elsewhere, the traditional boundaries that separate voice, video and data transmission services. Broadband technologies have now enabled telephone companies, data transmission service providers and cable-based broadcasters to enter each other's domains by offering voice, data and video services.

At first, the MII planned to build a unified broadband network for Shanghai's Pudong area, the new financial district tagged China's 'Manhattan'. In April 1999, the plan was, however, directly challenged by the entry of a new operator, China Netcom Corporation (CNC). The company, which has Jiang Mianheng, the son of Chinese President Jiang Zemin on its board, started as a joint venture among the Chinese Academy of Sciences (with Junior Jiang as its Vice Dean), the Shanghai Municipal Government, State Administration of Radio, Film and Television (SARFT) and the Ministry of Railways (MOR). It was created to provide a high-speed voice and data service in 15 cities, and to connect with 70 countries.[3] To do so, it planned to build its own broadband network. The immense political clout of this new entrant immediately circumvented the ministry's endeavour to avoid repeated construction of basic networks. Netcom's ambitious project, interestingly enough, was not endorsed by the MII, but by the State Development and Planning Commission (SDPC) under the State Council.[4]

In the same month of Netcom's launch, the SARFT vowed to set up the 'China Cable Television Networks Corporation', a national cable television company jointly formed by various regional CATV stations. The SARFT made rapid progress in creating a national network with more than a dozen provinces on a single network. Another 20 provincial trunk networks were also quickly built. This national network intended to introduce digital broadcasts featuring dozens of channels, and allow cheaper and faster Internet access than is possible over telephone lines (Rothman and Barker, 1999). Despite the strong desire by the SARFT to upgrade the cable infrastructure so that it can carry two-way voice and data traffic as well as television, its turf war with the MII has prevented it from doing so. Each of the rivals, the MII and the SARFT, has banned the other's industry from competing in its patch. With the exception of Shanghai, China's telecom and cable infrastructures duplicate each other.[5]

Within weeks, the Jitong Corporation also announced its plan to develop its own broadband network. In June 1999, the MOR aired its decision to set up a public phone company, the 'Railway Communications Information Group' (the Railcom), to provide public communications services by utilizing its railway-based nationwide fixed-line telecom network.

Other government agencies and government-linked companies also played their own tunes with little regard for the MII's regulatory authority. China International Trust and Investment Corporation (CITIC), an influential government-linked investment conglomerate, was reported to have laid thousands of miles of expensive fibre-optic cables around China in the late 1990s without getting permission from the MII. Such a blunt violation of regulations was backed by the conglomerate's connections in the Communist Party.[6]

Fighting for Broadband

Facing these challenges, the MII fought back by tightening its grip over the broadband network development. In April 2001, the MII and the SDPC jointly issued a notice demanding an immediate halt to unauthorized long-distance fibre-optic cable projects. All departments and enterprises that were not authorized to operate basic telecom businesses but owned long-distance fibre-optic network resources had to report to the MII and the SDPC within 30 days of the notice. The notice also reiterated that entities from foreign countries, as well as Hong Kong, Macau and Taiwan, were not allowed to make any direct investment in telecom network construction, operation and management before China joined the World Trade Organization (WTO).[7]

In June 2001, the MII issued a notice on a trial period for the opening of residential broadband markets in 13 Chinese cities. Eligible non- infrastructure telecom operators other than China Telecom and China Unicom could enter the residential broadband market. The trial sites included Beijing, Shanghai, Chongqing, Guangzhou, Shenzhen, Jinan, Qingdao, Wuhan, Nanjing, Hangzhou, Ningbo, Xiamen and Chengdu. The MII stipulated that from the date of the notice, companies that had already built or were building residential broadband networks in the cities other than the trial sites would have to discontinue the construction or operation of their networks. Other telecom operators would not be allowed to connect the networks of unapproved companies to the backbone networks.[8]

These notices, however, did not stop Netcom from advancing into the backbone network business. In April 2000, the MII appeased Netcom by opening the IP telephone market to the new carriers, among which were China Unicom, China Telecom and Jitong. The broadband network business was virtually open to all these old and new players.

Online Games

Confusions and conflicts of interests also arise in the area of Internet regulation. As the primary regulator for the info-communications industry, the MII has been the authorized agency to review, approve and grant operation licences to Internet service providers (ISPs). In 1999, the MII and its provincial post and telecom administrations (PTAs) approved more than 300 ISPs, among which 53 were approved for nationwide services.[9] Internal pressure from different Chinese governmental bodies, however, prompted the MII to relinquish its control over some sections in the field of the Internet. In an interview in December 1999, Wu Jichuan, the Minister of the MII, stated, 'Internet service providers will be regulated by the Ministry of Information Industry. Internet content providers will be regulated by other government agencies'. With regard to e-commerce, 'more government agencies will have to be involved'.[10]

Aside from the MII, a number of other governmental agencies are involved in the Internet regarding specific functions. As observed by Wang (2001):

> The Ministry of Public Security has indicated it has the authority to regulate Internet activities to ensure social stability. The State Secrecy Bureau has demonstrated its willingness to regulate the Internet by promulgating the State Secrets Protection Regulations for Computer Information Systems on the Internet in December 1999. The State Encryption Administration Commission was specifically created to oversee the manufacture, use, import, and export of encryption products. The State Administration for Industry and Commerce has issued numerous rules governing the registration of online e-commerce activities.

4.2   CONTAIN OR PROMOTE COMPETITION

Under the strategy for 'breaking up the monopoly and introducing competition', the MII continues to face a dilemma of its role. As a supposed-to-be impartial regulator, its primary goal should be promoting competition for the sake of consumer welfare and ensure a level playing field for the competing service providers. As a ministry overseeing the state-owned telecom players, however, it also has a paternalist concern about the profitability of these industrial players.

As discussed in Chapter 3, the MII tried to orchestrate guided competition in the telecom sector according to its agenda in the late 1990s. After the first ('vertical') divestiture of China Telecom in 1999 along business lines, the MII-guided competition was introduced to several sub-markets in the telecom sector with strictly divided business territories. These sub-markets include long-distance service (China Telecom versus Unicom), mobile telephony (China Mobile versus Unicom), local fixed-line service (mainly China Telecom, with Unicom in a few cities) and IP telephony (four licences were issued to China Telecom, Jitong, Unicom and Netcom in 2000). Such a vertically divided market structure was supposed to ensure limited competition that would not seriously threaten these carriers' profitability. With the entry of Netcom in 1999, various players have hence started several inter-regional broadband network projects, competing with each other in the business of backbone network construction.

Competition among the domestic carriers has, however, escalated to a level that the MII feels nervous about. As the competition intensifies, it has been caught in a dilemma between its duty to promote competition and its concerns over the revenue loss of the state-owned carriers, especially those which were formerly affiliated with the ministry.

One case illustrating the dilemma is the MII's intervention to halt a price war between China Mobile and China Unicom. After the ministry's two-year efforts to beef up Unicom in 1999–2000, the carrier became an effective rival to China Mobile, the mobile business spin-off of the former China Telecom group (see Chapter 3). With permission to launch short-term promotions, the two mobile carriers very soon started offering rates below state-sanctioned levels to lure new customers. By October 2001, however, the MII intervened by ordering the two mobile operators to halt the escalating price war between them. Su Jinsheng, director of the ministry's Telecommunications Administration, stressed that the government would continue to set basic telecom charges, including monthly service fees and mobile-phone calling charges. He emphasized that telecom operators had no right to modify these charges and the government must approve their promotion plans beforehand. He warned that the most severe punishment to those telecom operators who engage in illegal pricing would be revocation of their telecom licences.[11] In January 2003, for instance, the Beijing Telecommunications Administration fined China Unicom RMB 300,000 (US$ 36,245) for tariff violations related to promotional packages offered on the carrier's GSM network.[12]

A second case is the MII's wavering policy towards the personal handyphone system (PHS, or commonly known by its advertised name '*Xiao Ling Tong*' in Chinese, which literally means 'little smart'). The technology is a quasi-mobile telephony that piggybacks on the existing fixed-line network and switch capacity. Compared to other mature mobile-phone systems such as the global system for mobile communications (GSM) and code division multiple access (CDMA), the PHS is characterized by many technical restraints such as low capacity, small radius of coverage by single base stations and many blind zones. The PHS technology was intended to spread worldwide, but quickly declined in Japan after it reached seven million subscribers. It was also reported to be a failure in some other countries such as Thailand.

China Telecom, however, introduced the system quietly in some small cities by the end of 1997 and early 1998. By the end of 2001, PHS telephony had become available in more than 100 cities and localities in 28 provinces, with over four million users. Around September 2002, the PHS users in China exceeded the threshold of 10 million, and were expected to surpass 12 million by the end of 2002,[13] compared to the 176 million GSM and CDMA mobile phone users by mid-2002.

The business success of *Xiao Ling Tong* appears to be a result of regulatory policy failure.[14] China Telecom, after its first divestiture, had a difficult time as competition was introduced into the telecom market. Although it continued to keep a monopoly control over local loops, the fixed-line subscription growth in many cities was slowing to a saturation point. Its long-distance revenue had been squeezed by the competition from Unicom's toll service and IP telephony, provided by Netcom, Jitong and Unicom. Its only hope of new revenue growth used to be broadband data communications. The hope, however, was dashed by the entry of Netcom and cable television companies with their ambitious network-building plans. Meanwhile, China Telecom had over 100 million local loop capacity, of which only 60 per cent was utilized. Rather than sitting on its hands watching China Mobile and Unicom divide the fast-growing pie of mobile telephone market, China Telecom bypassed the regulatory barrier by launching *Xiao Ling Tong*, a quasi-mobile telephony, without a mobile phone licence issued by the MII.

The quasi-mobile telephony has a unique niche in the telecom market. On the supply side, since providing PHS telephony uses China Telecom's idle network capacity, the starting investment for the launch of the service is moderate. Part of the radio spectrum it uses coincides with that reserved for the third-generation (3G) mobile telephony, which had not been launched by 2002. It is expected that the 3G is unlikely to be widely used by 2005; by then the investment in the PHS should be more than reclaimed by revenue.[15] Meanwhile, China Telecom also hopes to convert the PHS customer base to mobile telephony once it obtains a mobile phone licence in future. On the demand side, *Xiao Ling Tong* is similar to a mobile phone, except for the lack of roaming function. Its call rate was only one-tenth of the mobile telephone rate in 2000–01, making it very attractive to low- and middle-income users.[16] The service thus has a well-targeted market segment, which represents 90 per cent of telephone users, who just use the mobile telephone within a local access and transport area (LATA), and 90 per cent of the mobile call traffic that incurs within the same local area.

Xiao Ling Tong's success has not only benefited China Telecom but has also brought in a huge fortune to UTStarcom, a small and fast-growing company in Silicon Valley, which has been the main supplier of the PHS technology to China. UTStarcom made its successful IPO on 3 March 2000 at NASDAQ. In the very same year, the company was selected by the magazine *Forbes* as one of the world's 20 most successful small companies (with an annual revenue below US$ 500 million) with a total annual sales revenue of US$ 368 million. In 2001, UTStarcom's global revenues amounted to US$ 627 million in which the China business accounted for 90 per cent. In August 2002, another business magazine, *Fortune*, selected UTStarcom as one of the 100 top Chinese companies listed in Mainland China, SAR Hong Kong, the US, London and Singapore.[17]

The success of the *Xiao Ling Tong* to China Telecom is a threat to the businesses of China Mobile and Unicom. In the latter's perspective, the launch of *Xiao Ling Tong* has resulted in redundant investment and the wasteful use of resources. For instance, China Mobile and China Unicom constructed a large GSM network in Lanzhou city, 50 per cent of its capacity being idle after satisfying the needs of local residents. The launch of *Xiao Ling Tong* in 2000 led to more idleness and waste of network resources for Mobile and Unicom.[18]

The fast growth of the PHS business has already seriously threatened the customer base of China Mobile and Unicom. In cities where the PHS is available, it has become a common practice for a mobile telephone subscriber to carry a PHS phone as well – he/she would use a mobile phone to make sure not to miss an incoming call even in the PHS phone's 'blind zones', but would only use a PHS phone to initiate or return calls to save calling costs. In Quanzhou city alone, of the 360,000 PHS users in 2001, 65 per cent were also subscribers of China Mobile or Unicom. Therefore, *Xiao Ling Tong*'s threat to mobile telephone carriers' revenue must be greater than as indicated by its relative customer base. It is no wonder that reports of *Xiao Ling Tong*'s expansion caused a slump of Unicom's share price in Hong Kong's stock market. Hostility to the PHS service prompted China Mobile and Unicom to block calls initiated from PHS numbers in some cities.[19] It was also reported that local China Telecom branches blocked mobile carriers' connection in retaliation to China Mobile's block on PHS connections.[20]

The MII's policy towards *Xiao Ling Tong* has been wavering. In May 2000, the ministry issued an order to halt the service nationwide for further reviews. Telecom enterprises were banned from constructing and operating a PHS without approval. The order caused an immediate slump of UTStarcom's share price, wiping out RMB 20 billion of its market value.[21] On 29 June 2000, however, the MII promulgated the 'Notice on Regulating PHS Development and Operation', which specifies the PHS as a 'supplement to and extension of fixed-line telephony', with 'small-scope, slow-mobility, and wireless connections to the network'. PHS business since then has become licensable.

China Telecom quickly interpreted the 'Notice' as a permit for its local branches to extend their fixed-line services to the PHS, despite the fact that China Mobile and Unicom argued that the PHS should be restricted to 'small scopes' like a campus or a residential neighbourhood. Following the 'Notice', an explosive growth of the PHS nevertheless swept across the country. Both China Mobile and Unicom claimed huge revenue loss due to the PHS competition.

On 21 November 2000, the MII issued a directive to *Xiao Ling Tong* providers, urging them to raise the monthly subscription fee to RMB 25–35. In February 2001, the MII again gave a directive that the PHS phone monthly subscription should be set either at RMB 25 with a per-minute rate of RMB 0.20 or at RMB 35 with a per-minute rate of RMB 0.15. Such administrative interventions clearly aimed to reduce the quasi-mobile phone's price advantage. The MII also banned the development of PHS in large cities.

However, many local telecom branches of China Telecom continued to charge PHS users at fixed-line rates despite the MII's order. Some even bypassed the ban on the business in large cities by providing the service in counties within large cities' administrative boundaries. It was once widely rumoured in October 2001 that the MII was soon to take back the PHS spectrums for 3G mobile phone development. The rumour, however, was quickly dismissed.

The wavering policy towards the PHS reflects the MII's policy dilemma. Its guided-competition policy attempts to minimize the erosion of revenue and profits by restricting the number of competitors and the manner of competitive behaviour. The paternalist concerns over the state-owned telecom giants' revenue has, however, not only gone against the regulator's duty to enhance consumer welfare through competition, but has also failed to reconcile the conflicting interests of these giant carriers under its care.

The MII's policy uncertainty may also be a reflection of the debate on this issue within the industry. Critics of the PHS pointed out the technological limits of the system and predicted that once the 3G-mobile phone is launched or China Telecom gets a real mobile phone licence, the PHS boom will soon lose its steam. Their advice is to restrict the PHS development to avoid 'wasteful investment' in this 'outdated technology' (Dai, 2002). In contrast, executives of UTStarcom expressed confidence in technological progress to overcome the limits of the PHS and to allow more value-added services – such as wireless fidelity (WiFi) service – for the system.[22] Some industrial gurus highlighted that it is not engineers but consumers who will determine the winning technology. In the IT communications industry, superior technology never guarantees business success. 'Low-tech' with a good market niche often wins.[23]

By 2003, the MII openly announced its stand towards *Xiao Ling Tong* to be 'neither encouraging nor intervening'.[24] Meanwhile it ordered the fixed-line operators to dismantle their city-wide wireless local loop operations based in the 450 MHz band using CDMA technology.[25] This move indicated the ministry's determination to draw a line between PHS and CDMA technologies and to contain *Xiao Ling Tong* service to be PHS-based. The 'no intervention' stand nevertheless allowed *Xiao Ling Tong* services to expand into major cities like Guangzhou, Beijing, Chongqing, and Shanghai by mid-2003.

4.3   THE RIVAL REGULATORS

With digital communication technology, cable television broadcasting and computer networks are converging into one industry. In optical fibre networks, the coaxial cable that delivers cable television and telephone lines that usually transmit phone calls and data are virtually interchangeable. A thrust of the US

Telecommunications Act 1996 is breaking up the legal barrier between the cable television service and telecom business. Such a convergence is also sanctioned in principle by China's 2001–05 Five-year Plan. However, this technological change has caused serious troubles for MII's regulatory authority.

One of the most intriguing issues in China's telecom sector is the rivalry between the MII, the telecom regulator and the SARFT, the regulator of broadcasting and television media. When the MII was set up in March 1998, it assumed regulatory powers over all public info-communications networks, which it interpreted to include CATV networks. The SARFT was assigned responsibility for the regulation and operation of the CATV networks. The relationship and balance of power between the MII and the SARFT are far from clear though. As observed by Rothman and Barker (1999):

> On the one hand, the broadcasting industry is no longer represented by a ministry-level entity, and crucial rule-making power has been placed, at least nominally, in the hands of MII. On the other hand, MII, unlike its predecessors (MPT and MEI), does not run the telephone companies it regulates: SARFT and its provincial and local affiliates retain control over MRFT's broadcasting facilities. Moreover, SARFT was not placed under MII, probably because SARFT is a special preserve of the Propaganda Department of the Communist Party, which has a particular interest in program content. … Although a 1997 State Council decree permitted MRFT to build a nationwide CATV link-up, State Council regulations that took effect in 1998 indicated that MRFT should use MPT's infrastructure to build the national network. In May 1998, SARFT announced its intention to proceed with construction of its national CATV network. The day after that announcement, MII publicly and forcefully stated its opposition. The result of this rivalry is that MII has been working on its own plan for a single, unified platform for all information industry service providers, while SARFT has proceeded with construction of its national network.

In the eyes of the MII, the SARFT's plan to build a national CATV network blatantly violated the ministry's authority over the nationwide network development. In 1999, however, despite the MII's opposition, the SARFT joined the force of several politically powerful players, including Netcom, Jitong, the MOR and CITIC (a government-linked investment conglomerate) to subsequently launch their own cross-region network projects.

With over 100 million subscribers, China is the world's largest cable television market. The SARFT has long been eager to enter the telecom market by using the cable infrastructure to provide a two-way voice, Internet connection and other communication services in addition to television broadcasting. The snag is that such a 'convergence' would be a zero-sum game between the telecom regulator and the media regulator, given the fact that the former still has a custodial role over the interests of key telecom carriers and the latter owns a network of cable television operators nationwide. On the one hand, the MII has ruled that cable television companies are not allowed to offer voice and Internet services unless they have an MII licence. On the other hand, the SARFT has countered by ruling that no telecom company can offer video content unless it is approved by the SARFT.[26]

The rivalry between telecom carriers under the MII and the SARFT's local affiliates can turn nasty. For instance, it was reported that, from 1997 to 2000, fierce conflicts between the television and telecom departments occurred in more than 40 counties and cities in the Hunan Province, causing over 100 casualties.[27] The conflict originated with both sides' reluctance to give up their cable television transmission. The war between the television and telecom departments began in 1997, when the provincial telecom department laid the multimedia communications network throughout the province. The Hunan television department accused the telecom department of unfair competition for granting 'free instalment and free reception of TV programmes' to approximately one million of its subscribers through the telecom network. The television department claimed that the 'preferential treatment' of the provincial telecom department directly caused more than RMB 20 million (US$ 2.4 million) in revenue loss to the provincial cable television department every year. Blood was shed when the two departments' competition to gain more customers intensified.

The following is the account of one of the bloody dramas that occurred in 1999:

> On May 15, 1999, the telecom bureau of Shaodong county hung banners that said 'TV programs transmitted by telecom multimedia have clear images and many channels to choose from' in the county seat and at all the townships. At 5 p.m., the staff of the county's cable TV station removed the banners from the streets. An hour later, more than 30 people from the telecom bureau charged into the Radio and TV Center with sticks and hammers. Zhao Shuangxi, deputy head of the radio and TV bureau, was seriously injured.
>
> Things were temporarily brought under control after police arrived at the scene. Approximately 10 minutes later, however, a dozen of the telecom employees came back to the radio and TV bureau in a military vehicle. They wounded more than 10 staff workers of the radio and TV department and cut all telephone lines in the building to prevent calls to the police.
>
> The police received news of the fight when a radio and TV department employee called from a public phone. They returned to quieten down the riot, and this time, stayed at the gate of the building instead of leaving. Another dozen telecom employees then made a third charge, forcing the gate open in their attempt to get inside.
>
> The police and officials of the county government formed a barricade to ward off the troublemakers, the newspaper said. The attack launched by the telecom

bureau was finally checked when the county government ordered reinforcements from the public security police and local militia.[28]

To break the deadlock, the MII put forward a 'mutual entry' proposal in July 2001. Zhang Chunjiang, the Vice Minister of the MII, suggested that the country should authorize the telecom network and cable television network to spread intersectional business under the same condition. The regulatory framework should permit the cable television operator to provide a telecom service while at the same time the telecom companies should communicate a cable television programme with its network resource.[29] The MII's proposal, however, was reported to have been declined by the SARFT.[30] An interesting development was that in the following weeks rumours fermented that the two regulatory bodies were to be dismantled to form a new state department similar to the US Federal Communications Commission (FCC). The rumour, which might reflect behind-the-curtain power turfs, was eventually dismissed by senior officials from both departments as groundless.[31]

As a Telecommunications Law is still absent, the MII's regulatory authority over the converged backbone network is still subject to challenges from various political-economic interests. This has been evident in the forced opening of a broadband network market by the political-business coalition of the SARFT, Netcom, Jitong and the MOR.

To alleviate the tensions and conflicts among various authorities, the State Council formed the National Informatization Leading Group in December 1999, chaired by Vice-Premier Wu Bangguo and vice-chaired by Minister Wu Jichuan of the MII. The group brought together concerned government entities to coordinate the development and management of national broadband networks, among other tasks (Wang, 2001). The relaunch of a super-ministerial coordination agency above the MII was an ominous reminiscence of the former JCSEI/NIISC task force that existed before the cabinet reshuffle at the 9th National People's Congress. This occurred a mere 21 months after the birth of the MII.

4.4   FIGHT FOR RULES

To fend off challenges to its domain and authority, the MII has been long fighting for a legal regulatory framework based on a basic *Telecommunications Law* in the hope that such a framework would put an end to the limbo. The conflicting interests amid the difficult regulatory issues in a fast-changing industry, however, have made the birth of such a law so far a difficult labour.

While a *Telecommunications Law* is still absent, the State Council approved and issued the MII-proposed *Telecommunications Regulations of the*

People's Republic of China in September 2000. This landmark legal document standardizes the regulatory framework for the telecom sector and unifies the existing regulations on tariffs, the issue of new licences, interconnections, network development and private/foreign participation. The document spells out major principles of exercising supervision and regulation over the industry in Article 4:

- Separating governmental functions from business operations;
- Eliminating monopoly, encouraging competition;
- Promoting development; and
- Being open, fair and just.

Article 3 clearly states that 'The department in charge of the information industry under the State Council is entitled to exercise supervision and regulation over the country's telecom industry in accordance with this set of regulations.' The rules divide telecom companies into two types. One is the basic telecom business operator who provides public network infrastructure, data and voice transmission services. The other is the value-adding telecom business operator who uses the public network to provide telecom and information services (Article 8).

All basic telecom business operators and the value-adding telecom business operators whose service scope covers two or more provincial territories must be licensed from 'the department in charge of the information industry under the State Council' (DII-SC). Other value-adding telecom business operators should be licensed by provincial telecom regulatory bodies (Article 9). A crucial requirement for a basic telecom business operator to be licensed is being a legally established corporation in which the state share or stake is no less than 51 per cent (the controlling stake). As for the value-adding telecom business operators, there is no specific requirement for state control, thus clearing the way for non-state and foreign players (Table 4.1, based on Articles 10 and 13).

To ensure fair access to the public network by the new entrants, the *Regulations* specify that interconnection between different networks should follow the principles of feasibility, economic rationale, justice and fairness and mutual cooperation (Article 17). According to the *Regulations*, a dominant telecom operator must not refuse the request for interconnection put forward by other telecom operators and specialized (non-public) network units (Article 17).

Under the *Regulations*, telecom tariffs consist of market-coordinated prices (set by service providers), government-guided prices (which are floating ranges allowed for operators to set their prices/rates), and government-set prices (for important tariff rates) (Article 24). Pricing is mainly cost-based. The DII-SC is authorized to play a pivotal role in government involvement in telecom tariff setting (Article 25).

Table 4.1   Types of telecom operators

Type of operator	Business scope	Licence authority	Requirement for state equity share
Basic telecom business operator	Provision of public network infrastructure, public data and voice transmission service	DII-SC	The state share or stake is no less than 51 per cent
Value-adding telecom business operator	Using the public network to provide telecom and information services	• DII-SC for those service scope covers two or more provincial territories • Provincial telecom regulatory bodies for others	No specific requirement

Source: *Telecommunications Regulations of the People's Republic of China* (September 2000).

The regulatory framework also reconfirms that 'the State shall implement a pay-for-use scheme for utilization of telecom resources based on unified planning, centralized management and rational allocation' (Article 27). These resources refer to radio frequencies, orbit locations of satellites and codes of telecom network. The operators' possession and usage of such resources will be levied by the state at rates suggested by the DII-SC and the fiscal departments of the State Council (Article 28).

Administrative assignment and public auction are referred to as the two measures to allocate the telecom resources (Article 29). Meanwhile, telecom operators should fulfil their obligations of providing a universal service, which are enforced through the DII-SC-specified assignments or tender clauses (Article 44).

Finally, the *Regulations* reaffirm the DII-SC's unified planning authority over the development of a public network, specialized (non-public) network and radio/television transmission network (Article 45). Projects of public telecom networks, specialized telecom networks and transmission networks for radio and television broadcasting must get approval from the DII-SC before they go through the state approval procedure for capital construction projects, as long as they involve nationwide information network projects or construction projects exceeding the state-defined quota. Telecom network's design, development and operation by any player must meet the requirements and standards of national security and network security (Article 61). With these rules in place, the DII-SC is set to keep its control over the investment and development of the country's telecom infrastructure.

Since the promulgation of the *Regulations*, a number of regulatory sub-rules have been issued to complement the basic framework. For instance, to allow a greater degree of competition and business autonomy for telecom operators, the SDPC and the MII jointly circulated a catalogue of telecom service fees to be 'market-coordinated' in July 2002. From then on, telecom operators have been allowed to set service rates/prices within the range of businesses specified by the catalogue. On month later, in a move to increase transparency of the government's role in telecom tariff and rate setting, the SDPC and the MII jointly promulgated two more important regulations in August 2002. One is the *Provisions of Approval and Filing Procedures of Telecom Service Rates*. The other is the *List of Telecommunications Service Rates to be Co-determined by Provincial Communications Administrations and the Provincial Price Regulatory Authorities*. [32] The two promulgated regulations specify the scope of businesses of which government-guided prices and government-set prices that should be co-determined by provincial authorities. With these specifications, the pricing of telecom businesses within the provincial jurisdictions has been delegated to provincial authorities. The MII continues to monitor the nationwide basic telecom service rates and is responsible for proposing adjustments for these rates to be approved by the State Council (Article 8 of the *Provisions*).

From the review of the above rules, it is tempting to conclude that the promulgation of the *Regulations* was a victory for the MII as it contributed to a crucial step to establish the ministry as the primary state regulatory authority overseeing the telecom industry. This is based on the logical interpretation of the term 'department in charge of information industry under the State Council' (DII-SC) as the equivalent of the MII. A consistent regulatory framework that places the MII as the central regulatory authority seems to have emerged and is ready to put an end to the lawlessness and arbitrariness of China's telecom sector.

The reality, however, is far more complicated. Even within the framework of the *Regulations*, the State Council and the MII still have to decide what to do with the fallow and technically illegal networks built by agencies like the CITIC. The promulgation of the *Regulations* did not end the turf wars between the MII and rival regulators. As we will see in Chapter 6, more recent developments have dramatically changed the landscape of China's telecom industry and its regulatory framework after 2000. A major cause of these changes was the opening of the market to foreign companies following China's acceptance as a member of the WTO.

Summary

Various interest groups, backed by powerful government ministries and departments, have been vying for controls over the telecom market. Their conflicts with the MII have featured the process of forming a regulatory regime in recent years. Such a situation is likely to continue as long as there are still rents not fully dissipated in the info-communications sector. Meanwhile, the MII has yet to solve the dilemma between being a paternalist caretaker of the state-owned telecom carriers and being a market umpire to ensure fair play and consumer welfare.

NOTES

1. *Hong Kong Economic Journal* (Hong Kong), 10 December 1999.
2. Interview with scholars of the Shanghai Institute of P & T Economy, 8 July 2000.
3. *South China Morning Post* (Hong Kong), 15 December 1999.
4. *China Telecom Weekly News* (Boston), 17–21 May 1999.
5. 'Chinese Telecoms: Into the Crucible', *The Economist* (UK), 1 November 2001.
6. 'Chinese Telecoms: Into the Crucible', *The Economist* (UK), 1 November 2001.
7. 'China tightens regulation of telecom projects', *China Online News*, 6 April 2001.
8. *Jisuanji Shijie Ribao* (*Computer World Daily*, China), 20 June 2001.
9. Xinhua News Agency, 16 February 2000, http://www.xinhua.org/chanjing.
10. 'Wu said China ISPs, ICPs regulated separately', *China Online News*, 17 December 1999, http://www.chinaonline.com.
11. 'MII strengthens regulation of telecom charges', *China Online News*, 25 October 2001.
12. 'China Unicom fined for tariff violations', Global Wireless.com, 17 January 2003.
13. '*Xiao Ling Tong* users exceeds 100 million', China Communications Net, http://www.c114.net/, 21 October 2002.

14. The account of the PHS development in the rest of this section is based on Gao (2002) and Dai (2002), if not noted otherwise.

15. It was reported that China Telecom had already fully recovered its RMB 600 million investment in PHS at Xi An City, with another RMB 400 million surplus by mid-2002 (China Communications Net, http://www.c114.net, 16 August 2002).

16. PHS call rate was RMB 0.20 per minute (one-way charge), monthly subscription was RMB 15 in 2002 (China Communications Net, http://www.c114.net, 16 August 2002).

17. 'UTStarcom Selected as Fortune's 100 Top Chinese listed companies', http://www.utstar.com.cn/news, 12 August 2002.

18. 'China Mobile, China Telecom argue over handyphone system in Lanzhou', *China Online News*, 21 August 2000.

19. 'Hand phone cannot call Xiao Ling Tong in Fuzhou', China Communications Net, http://www.c114.net, 11 October 2002.

20. 'China Mobile, China Telecom argue over handyphone system in Lanzhou', *China Online News*, 21 August 2000.

21. '*Xiao Ling Tong*'s resurrection', China Communications Net, http://www.c114.net, 11 September 2002.

22. '*Xiao Ling Tong*'s resurrection', China Communications Net, http://www.c114.net, 11 September 2002.

23. 'About the debate on Xiao Ling Tong: an editorial comment', *Youdian Jingji* (P & T Economy), 2002, 58 (1), p. 16.

24. 'Wu Jichuan interprets MII stand to Xiao Ling Tong', Communications Net, http://www.c114.net, 10 March 2003.

25. 'China's MII bans CDMA-based WLL systems', *Global Wireless.com* 28 March 2003.

26. 'China's tangled broadband revolution', *Financial Times* (FT.com), 1 August 2001.

27. The report on this event is based on 'Fights over cable TV transmission in Hunan leave more than 100 casualties', *China Online News*, 1 August 2000.

28. Ibid.

29. 'Wire TV operator will be allowed to enter into telecom', *Asiainfo Daily China News*, 20 July 2001.

30. 'Cable authorities decline telecoms sector's plan to converge markets', www.moftec.gov.cn, 24 July 2001.

31. 'MII denies tie-up of information, broadcasting ministries', *Asiainfo Daily China News*, 8 August 2001.

32. Ministry of Information Industry website, http://www.mii.gov.cn/.

5. The impact of China's WTO membership

On 12 November 2001 China formally signed an accord with the World Trade Organization (WTO) to become the WTO's 143rd member on 11 December 2001. This marked the ending of China's 15-year-long marathon endeavour to join the organization. The event was hailed as the 'greatest leap forward in the history of the WTO' according to the European Union (EU) Trade Commissioner Pascal Lamy, as it brought 22 per cent of the world's population, and the most dynamic developing economy, into the rule-based global trading system.[1]

As a result of the negotiations on conditions for its accession, China has agreed to undertake a series of important commitments to open and liberalize its trade and investment regime in order to be better integrated in the .world economy and offer a more predictable environment for trade and investment in accordance with WTO rules. Most tariffs and many of the trade barriers are to be lowered or removed. Foreign-funded enterprises will have a better chance to gain 'national treatment' in many industries that used to be closed to foreign participation.

Implementation of these commitments will effectively increase the accessibility of China's domestic market to foreign businesses and put an end to the many protections provided by the government's industrial policy regime for the indigenous companies. Fiercer competition is expected with foreign goods and firms, which will threaten the survival of those less efficient indigenous players. It is therefore no wonder that the Chinese media has frequently compared the post-WTO influx of foreign competition to the invasion of a 'sheep colony' by 'hungry wolves'.[2] For the telecom industry, the severity of the challenges is no less since this sector had been until recently one of the most protected sectors in the Chinese economy.

5.1   THE CLOSED YEARS

China's accession to the WTO paves the way for foreign equity investment in this sector. This has changed a long-standing official policy that prohibited foreign involvement in management and equity investment in the telecom service sector. A full statement of the policy can be found in the announcement made by the former Ministry of Post and Telecommunications (MPT) on 25 May 1993: 'no organization, enterprise or individual outside China may engage in the management of China's broadcasting networks, special wire or wireless services, or become a shareholder in a telecommunications business.'[3]

As part of China's industrial policy regime, the State Council promulgated the *Catalogue of Industries for Guiding Foreign-funded Investment* in June 1995,[4] which was later revised in December 1997.[5] The 1995 catalogue covers 315 sectors and the 1997 catalogue, which took effect on 1 January 1998, covers several hundred products and technologies in 29 industries. In principle, the government divided foreign-invested projects into four categories: namely, projects to be encouraged, projects to be allowed, projects to be restricted and projects to be forbidden.

Projects to be encouraged included those that:

- involve new agricultural techniques, comprehensive agriculture development, and development of energy, transportation and major raw materials;
- involve new and/or high-tech and thus can help save energy and raw materials, raise the technical level and economic efficiency;
- can meet the demand of the international market and help upgrade products and thus help open up markets and expand exports;
- involve new technology and equipment for the comprehensive use of natural resources, and recycling of resources and prevention of environmental pollution;
- can provide better use of manpower and natural resources in the central and western parts of the country, and are in accord with the state industrial policies; and
- are encouraged by state regulations or policies.

Projects to be encouraged can enjoy a range of preferential treatment as stipulated by state laws and administrative regulations. In addition, if the projects are connected with the construction and operation of energy and transportation infrastructure (coal, electricity, local railways, roads and ports) that require large investment and have long reimbursement periods, investors can expand their business scope to related areas upon state approval.

Manufacturing and production of the following telecom-related products and systems fall into the 'encouraged' category:

- satellite communications systems;

- digital cross-connection systems;
- digital communications multi-media system equipment;
- access network communications system equipment;
- new-tech equipment that supports communications networks;
- integrated services digital network (ISDN); and
- information, communications, networking technology.

Projects to be restricted include those:

- with technologies that have been well developed domestically or already introduced from abroad; or projects that would add to a domestic production capacity that has already well satisfied domestic demand;
- in sectors that are only open for foreign investment on a trial basis or are under a state monopoly franchise;
- involving prospecting and exploiting rare and precious mineral resources;
- involving industries under state-unified planning; and
- being restricted by state laws and administrative regulations.

Restricted projects are to have a definite term of operation. In the case of a joint venture, the fixed assets put in by the Chinese side should come from the Chinese firm's own capital or assets (without using bank loans or relying on raised funds). Telecom-related products in the 'restricted' category include satellite television receivers and key components, digital program-controlled area-wide and customer switchboard.

Foreign investment is prohibited for projects that fall into any of the following categories:

- Projects that endanger the country's security or social and public interest;
- Projects that would cause environmental pollution or bring harm to natural resources and human health;
- Projects that have to occupy large tracts of farm land, are harmful to environment protection and development of land resources, and/or endanger the security of military facilities and their effective uses;
- Projects that have to use China's own special craftsmanship or indigenous skills for production;
- Other projects that are banned by the state law and administrative regulations.

Projects not belonging to the categories of being encouraged, restricted or forbidden are those in the 'allowed' category. In both 1995 and 1997 Catalogues, the 'operation and management of postal and telecom services' are put under the 'prohibited' category.

Thanks to the ban, before China became a member of the WTO, foreign participants were prohibited from holding a direct equity position in Chinese telecom service companies. They had also been barred from having any operational control without the approval of the State Council, which was resolute in refusing to do so.

As a result, foreign involvement had been limited to arm's-length agreements, wherein foreign companies discreetly provide investment in exchange for a share of operating revenue (Hsu, 1999). However, even such forms of involvement were not tolerated by the MII as shown in the case of the so-called 'China-China-Foreign' (CCF) joint ventures.

Foreign investors had a short-lived optimism in 1995–98 when China Unicom, in a pressing need for start-up capital, roped in 45 foreign companies to take US$ 1.4 billion worth of indirect equity stakes in its operations through the CCF joint ventures. Under the 'CCF' model, a 'China-Foreign' joint venture is formed between a local company and a foreign firm, routing the funds through the joint venture into the network operator (for example Unicom). The deal opened a loophole in regulations barring foreign companies from operating a domestic telephone network and allowed them to earn money officially on installation and 'consulting' fees. De facto foreign equity could reach as high as 90 per cent.

By the end of that year, however, the Ministry of Information Industry (MII) officials branded the joint ventures 'irregular' and accused them of reaping profits at the expense of government programmes designed to subsidize telephone service in poor and remote regions.[6] Consequently in 1999 the MII forced China Unicom to wind up its initial commercial agreements with foreign investors in these projects. The foreign companies, which included Deutsche Telekom, France Telecom, Spring, NTT International and Bell Canada, had to renegotiate in order to retrieve their investments.[7]

The only glaring point during this period was AT&T winning a joint venture project to build and operate an IP network in Pudong, Shanghai, in May 1999: the first time a foreign operator had been allowed to offer telecom services in its own right. The deal was kept in a low profile as a pilot project sanctioned by the MII.

5.2   RELUCTANCE TO OPEN

China's reluctance to open its telecom service sector to foreign equity investment and participation in the 1990s was based on several considerations. These include the protection for a strategic industry and its indigenous carriers, national security and sovereignty, and the need to maintain political stability and ideological control.

As discussed in Chapter 2, the telecom sector's spectacular achievements from the mid-1980s to the late 1990s were a result of growth-oriented incentive structure embedded in a well-protected monopolistic business. A variety of preferential state industrial policies were indispensable to the success of launching the industry into a fast-growing track. Given that, there was a legitimate concern that the government's preferential policy to support the telecom sector could be taken advantage of by the foreign players if their entry were to be allowed. 'For foreign companies investing in telecommunications operations, profits have been to a great extent attributable to preferential policies offered by the state', lamented an MII official in 1998.[8]

A related concern was the fear that an early opening to foreign participation would undermine the MPT/MII plans to extend a universal service of telecom to the population in rural and remote regions. According to Wu Jichuan, the Minister of MII, much work remained to be done to provide more Chinese with access to basic telecom services. By 1999, nearly a quarter of administrative villages still had no access to plain-old telephone lines.[9] A huge disparity in telecom development has existed among different regions. Even in coastal provinces with the highest telephone penetration rate, the digital gap between the urban and rural residents has been large. To provide a universal service in a low-income country with a huge regional disparity, some extent of cross-subsidization in the tariff structure would be inevitable. Such a rate structure is usually featured by the cross-subsidization provided by overpriced long-distance services to underpriced local services; by urban users to rural users; and by high-traffic areas to low-traffic areas. This structure, however, would be vulnerable to new entrants who were set to 'cream-skim' the lucrative part of the market. In such a situation, a premature opening of the market to competition would endanger the efforts to provide a universal service to residents in rural and underdeveloped regions.

To understand the effects of these concerns on policy making, it is useful to introduce a game-theory framework used by Mueller and Lovelock (2000) to analyse how national interest was defined and played out in the Chinese government's policies towards foreign equity investment and participation in the telecom service sector. There are four players in this 'game': the 'state', the 'China Telecom group', the 'competitors', which refers to the indigenous carriers that compete with the China Telecom group and the 'foreign strategic investors'. With respect to the telecom sector, the State wants to maximize the sector's contribution to the overall economic development while minimizing its own expense. It treats China Telecom as an instrument for building up the nation's telecom infrastructure and providing universal services.

China Telecom, as a state-owned enterprise with a privileged dominance in the industry, wants to retain its privileged status as a national champion and instrument of development. It is also keen to shelter its rates and revenue streams from competition and to stop foreign direct investment (FDI) that would beef up its competitors. Given the state-selected policy, China Telecom can decide either to follow a growth strategy (G) by single-mindedly focusing on meeting infrastructure build-out targets set by the state or to follow a profit-making strategy (P) by focusing more on profitability and productivity but less on growth. The indigenous players, with political-economic interests to secure their right in this profitable market, can choose either to stay on and compete with China Telecom or to exit. As for foreign investors (FI), whose interest lies in profit opportunities in the Chinese market, the options include investment with equity (E) if allowed, investment without equity (I) and stay out with no investment (O).

The market structure can take any of these four forms: (1) growth-oriented competition (GC), in which China Telecom pursues the growth strategy and indigenous competitors remain in the market and complement China Telecom while pressuring it to become more efficient; (2) profit-oriented competition (PC), in which China Telecom becomes profit-oriented while the indigenous competitors remain in the market; (3) growth-oriented monopoly (GM), in which China Telecom retains its status as a growth instrument but indigenous competitors exit the market; and (4) profit-oriented monopoly (PM), in which China Telecom reorients towards profit (thereby abandoning its status as a development instrument and focusing on profitable localities) and domestic competitors exit the market. It is easy to expect that the state would rank its preferences for these structures as GC > PC > GM > PM.

Meanwhile, the state may choose among three moves towards foreign investment: keep the ban on foreign equity investment but allow other forms of investments; open the sector partially to foreign equity investment without allowing foreigners a controlling share of equity; and open the sector fully to foreign investors by allowing foreigners controlling shares. Due to the concerns over national sovereignty and the need to utilize foreign capital, the ranking of the state's preferences for foreign investment is: investment without equity (I) > investment with equity (E) > no investment (O).

On the other hand, under the ban or partial opening for equity investment, the foreign investors would prefer staying out (O) if indigenous competitors are absent. They would prefer investment without equity (I) only when indigenous competitors are present as long as foreign equity investment (E) is banned. Otherwise they would always prefer to invest with equity (E).

Meanwhile, without foreign investment, the indigenous competitors would always exit the market since they would not have enough capital to compete with China Telecom. A full open market with too much foreign competition with equity investment would also force indigenous competitors out. Otherwise they would stay and compete. As for China Telecom, since the growth strategy increases its political status and rationale for privileges, it would always prefer a growth strategy to a profit strategy unless it was exposed to equity-investment-based foreign competition under a full open market.

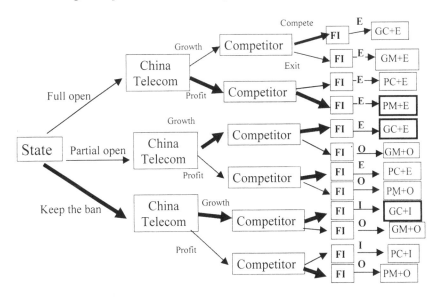

Note: The thicker arrow refers to the player's choice; FI = 'foreign investors'.

Source: Based on Mueller and Lovelock (2000).

Figure 5.1   State policy options for opening the telecom market for foreign investors

Given these assumptions, Mueller and Lovelock (2000) use a 'backward induction' approach to derive the sub-game perfect equilibria of this game, as illustrated by Figure 5.1. These sub-game perfect equilibria allow the state to anticipate the outcomes of the different policy options: (a) a full open policy would lead to the 'PM+E' outcome, a profit-oriented monopoly with foreign equity investment; (b) a partial open policy would lead to the 'GC+E' outcome, a growth-oriented competition with foreign equity investment; and (c) a continuous ban on equity investment would lead to the 'GC+I' outcome, a growth-oriented competition with non-equity foreign investment. With the state's preference ranking, it was no wonder that the government kept its ban on foreign equity investment throughout the 1990s. As stated by the authors, 'the model predicts that, absent any pressure to join WTO and responding only domestic policy concerns and the behaviour of foreign investors, China would keep its telecommunication service market closed to foreign direct investment.'

Apart from these payoffs, the reluctance to open the telecom sector also arose from national security concerns. The Ministry of National Security has always been concerned about the potential threat to communications security and sovereignty once foreign companies are allowed to operate China's telecom network. In other countries, concerns over national security in communications have also arisen when foreign players entered. For instance, concern over Australia's national security was a major hurdle in Singapore Telecom's (SingTel) bid to take over Cable and Wireless Optus, one of the two main Australian telecom carriers, in September 2001.[10] Given China's century-long history of being intimidated and invaded by foreign powers, such a concern is understandable.

5.3   BOTTOM LINES: INDUSTRIAL VERSUS NATIONAL

Despite the government's preference for 'growth-oriented competition with non-equity foreign investment', the policy towards foreign investment in the telecom sector has to be part of the national strategy of long-term development. To the Chinese leadership, joining the WTO is a strategic move necessary for achieving the government's grand plan to make China the largest developed economy by the mid-twenty-first century.

National Stakes in WTO Membership

Becoming a WTO member, China is set to benefit from several aspects. First, WTO membership secures China's trade relationship with the rest of the world on multinational legal terms. Before accession to the WTO, China used to rely on the bilateral relationships to shape its trade with major trading partners. Such relationships can be fickle and uncertain, subject to shocks of non-economic events, increasing risks for producers and investors, and demanding a huge investment of time and effort by government officials to negotiate and administer them.

With WTO membership, China can replace the bilateral relationships with its largest trade partners by a single, multilateral trade relationship with the rest of the world.

> The multilateral trade relationship provided by the WTO is far less costly and more permanent. It is defined by the WTO rules and the WTO's dispute settlement system for enforcing those rules. The rules are legally binding upon each member, and they require from each member a solemn commitment to respect and to implement the rule of law. (Eglin, 2003)

The economic security brought in by such a relationship is crucial to sustain China's economic growth. As pointed out by McKibbin and Woo (2002), deficit spending and exports are the two growth engines that have kept China's GDP growth rates above 7 per cent since the mid-1990s. China's weak fiscal position, however, makes deficit spending a non-sustainable engine of growth.

> The present fiscal situation is marked by the constant need to recapitalize the state banks, the need to fund future pension claims, and the inability of the government to increase revenue collection substantially. Hence, if export is also not a sustainable engine of growth, then a drastic slowdown in growth is inevitable. The United States is China's biggest export market. … Clearly, in order for exports to be a sustainable growth engine, China must secure assured access to its biggest market. And, only WTO membership can prevent the United States from the impulsive unilateral action of switching off one of China's most important growth engines by simply denying MFN status to China in any year.

The second benefit of being a WTO member comes from the protection the WTO rules will provide for China's trade rights and the expectations of its exporters, against damaging protectionist policies in overseas markets. Along with China's success in increasing its exports over the past 20 years, China's vulnerability to discriminatory, ad hoc protectionism in its major export markets has grown.

> Were this to continue, and perhaps escalate in the future if world economic growth were to suffer a serious decline, it could prove a major set-back to China's economic growth and development, and even to China's economic reform process. Once WTO accession is complete, China's exporters will more confidently be able to make long-term business decisions on the expansion of their activities. The more open the Chinese economy becomes, the more China will benefit from the legal security of the rules-based trading system. (Eglin, 2003)

A third benefit that has arisen from China's membership in the WTO is the opportunity to air its own voice in future WTO negotiations. As the world's sixth largest exporter, China certainly could pursue its own trade interests vigorously in these negotiations and contribute to the rule-making process of the international trade regime.

With China as a WTO member, major trading powers have to lift discriminating trade restrictions imposed on its exports. The removal of trading barriers sets to increase China's exports, especially in the textile and garment industries, which account for 20 per cent of the country's total export volume.

Last but not least, as pointed out by many observers, the most important benefit for China to become a member of WTO is that the process will 'lock China on to the path of deepening economic reform' to the direction of "a prototype WTO economy"' (Woo, 2001).

> It will 'lock-in', in other words, the accumulated trade reform process that the Chinese government has undertaken to date, and provide a platform from which China can sustain its reform process into the future. ... By placing China's reforms within the broader context of trade liberalization by all WTO Members, it can increase the returns to trade reform in China through reciprocal market access abroad, and help the Chinese Government to resist pressure domestically to reverse the process of reform. (Eglin, 2002)

'The principles of WTO provide China with direction, contents, procedures, disciplines, and commitment for the search of best institutions' (Xiao and Zhou, 2000). When China has to act in accordance with international practices defined by WTO rules, foreign investors will feel more confident about conducting business with China. Such confidence will no doubt translate into higher foreign investments in China.

Predominated by these expected benefits, China was ready to revamp its industrial policies to meet the terms and conditions of joining the WTO. To withstand the anticipated shock brought about by opening the telecom sector for foreign competition, the Chinese government has adopted the following strategies:

1. Negotiate for caps and geographic restrictions on foreign ownership and for a longer time period for removing the caps and restrictions during the WTO deal making.
2. Reform the telecom market structure by encouraging domestic competition to pre-empt 'cream-skimming' opportunities for foreign entrants after accession to the WTO.
3. Beef up the domestic carriers' financial strength and competitiveness by listing them in overseas stock markets.
4. Prepare a legal framework that ensures state control over a basic network.

Industrial Bottom Line

The first strategy was actively pursued during the 15-year long negotiation process (1987–2001) for China's WTO membership. On China's road to the WTO membership, the US acted as the major gatekeeper that set terms on China's joining the international trading body. It is now history how tenaciously the Chinese negotiators were pushing for more favourable accession terms through the Marathon endeavour, especially in negotiations with their US and EU counterparts.

The opening of China's telecom sector for foreign investment was one of the issues for tough bargaining. As discussed earlier, throughout the 1990s, China imposed some of the world's tightest restrictions on foreign investment in the telecom services. Compared to China's overall policy of attracting and encouraging FDI in its economy, the draconian restriction on foreign equity investment in the telecom service sector was exceptional.

In April 1999, in his failed bid to wrap up a deal with the US, Chinese Premier Zhu Rongji offered for the first time up to 49 per cent foreign ownership of basic telecom services and 51 per cent foreign ownership for value-added and paging services within four years. Some overseas media sniffed a policy rift between Zhu, the Prime Minister and Wu Jichuan, the Minister of Information Industry.

'Neither Americans nor Europeans could agree to China's WTO accession without a greatly liberalised telecoms market, an end that Mr Zhu also seeks, and which Mr Wu faces pressure to endorse', reported *The Economist.*[11] Rumours were rife that Mr Wu was so unhappy with the offer that he even threatened to resign if the offer was not modified.[12] Whether these rumours carry any truth or not, it is interesting to note that, in November 1999 when China and the US finally sealed the deal, the maximum foreign ownership allowed for value-added and ICP services was capped at 50 per cent while the 49 per cent cap for all other services was to be kept as a major safeguard for Chinese shareholders' controlling stakes (Table 5.1).

The Sino–European Union accord on China's WTO entry (signed in May 2000) further accelerates the opening in mobile telephony in two years after the accession. Foreign ownership of up to 25 per cent was to be allowed upon accession, 35 per cent after one year and 49 per cent after three years. Leasing and resale of telecom circuits will be allowed for foreign firms in three years.[13]

Let us return to the three sub-game perfect equilibria displayed in Figure 5.1 under three policy scenarios. Now since the WTO entry has ruled out the option of banning equity investment by foreigners, the outcome (c), a growth-oriented competition with non-equity foreign investment, is no longer feasible. The 'second-best' outcome to the state is then (b), the scenario in which a partial open policy without allowing foreigners a controlling share of equity leads to a growth-oriented competition with foreign equity investment. The final WTO deal ensures the industry's bottom line: China will not permit more than 49 per cent of foreign ownership in basic telecom services (fixed line and mobile) even six years after its WTO accession. This is to make sure that foreign investors will be partners rather than competitors of the domestic carriers.

Table 5.1   Sino-US agreement on China's accession to the WTO: timetable for opening the telecom market

Maximum percentage of foreign ownership allowed and geographic limitations for joint-ventures in telecom sector		
Value-added and paging services		
Upon accession	30	Beijing, Shanghai and Guangzhou
1 year after accession	49	The above plus the 14 major cities
2 years after accession	50	Nationwide
Mobile services		
1 year after accession	25	Beijing, Shanghai and Guangzhou
3 years after accession	35	The above plus the 14 major cities
5 years after accession	49	Nationwide
Fixed-line services		
3 years after accession	25	Beijing, Shanghai and Guangzhou
5 years after accession	35	The above plus the 14 major cities
6 years after accession	49	Nationwide
Internet content providers (ICP)		
Upon accession	30	Beijing, Shanghai and Guangzhou
1 year after accession	49	The above plus the 14 major cities
2 years after accession	50	Nationwide
Internet service providers (ISP)		
3 years after accession	25	Beijing, Shanghai and Guangzhou
5 years after accession	35	The above plus the 14 major cities
6 years after accession	49	Nationwide

Note: The 14 major cities are Chengdu, Chongqing, Dalian, Fuzhou, Hangzhou, Nanjing, Ningbo, Qingdao, Shenyang, Shenzhen, Xiamen, Xian, Taiyuan and Wuhan.

Source: The Economist Intelligence Unit, *Telecoms & Wireless Asia*, 14 January 2000.

Reduce Creams for Skimming

The second strategy to promote domestic competition emerged during the early 1990s amid mounting domestic pressures from some non-MPT interests. Several years of tussles for power gave birth to a regulatory regime centred around the MII. Guided by the MII, the industry underwent in the late 1990s major restructures featured by the divestiture of China Telecom along business lines and the beefing-up of its major rival, China Unicom (see Chapter 3 for details). In this process, the telecom sector in the late 1990s witnessed a series of reforms that featured opening, tariff revamping and the formulation and completion of telecom legislation. Special efforts were made to reduce the degree of cross-subsidizing in telephone service rates. From 1995 to 1999, the installation fee for a fixed phone line was cut from RMB 300–5000 to below RMB 800. The mobile telephone's access charge was reduced by 75 per cent. In the second half of the 1990s, international direct dial (IDD) rates dropped by 60–70 per cent. Internet access fee decreased by 70–80 per cent (Qian and Zhang, 2000).

In December 2000, the MII, the SDPC and the Ministry of Finance jointly announced massive cuts in telecom and Internet charges, slashing some fees by more than 50 per cent, with effect from January 2001.[14] For fixed-line phone rates, fee-cutting measures included: changing the local telephone-charging unit from three minutes to one; slashing the monthly service subscription for a fixed-line telephone from RMB 24 (US$ 2.90) to RMB 18 (US$ 2.17); and abolishing the fixed-line telephone installation fees. Meanwhile, the price to lease circuits from China Telecom was lowered to 72.8 per cent; mobile phone networking access fees was abolished; and the Internet connection fee was reduced to RMB 0.02 (US$ 0.002) per minute. Domestic and international rates were further slashed by 50 per cent. The IDD rate cut further squeezed the market for the long-distance services provided by the Internet protocol (IP) telephony, which was started in April 2000.

Rate slashing and competition from IP telephony have already eaten into the most 'creamy' part of China Telecom's revenue – the long-distance telecom service. According to a study conducted by Pyramid Research, long-distance revenue per fixed line in China is projected to drop from US$ 38 in 2002 to US$ 24 by 2006.[15] Thanks to fierce competition between China Mobile and Unicom, the rapid expansion of the mobile telecom market has already reached a point when both carriers see their average revenue per user (ARPU) dropping dramatically. These trends meet well with the government's strategy to pre-empt the cream-skimming opportunities for foreign entrants after China's WTO accession.

5.4   PRE-EMPTIVE MOVES

Listing Indigenous Carriers Overseas

After signing the Sino–US agreement on China's WTO accession in November 1999, the MII accelerated the pace of arrangements for the major Chinese carriers to tap the Hong Kong and other overseas capital markets. In May 2000, the MII arranged for the China Mobile Communications (Group) Corporation to become the 100 per cent owner of the China Telecom (Hong Kong) Company by acquiring at no cost the 43 per cent stake in CT (HK) from the China Telecom Group Corporation. After changing its name to the China Mobile (HK) Company, the giant-listed company in Hong Kong's stock market started preparations to purchase seven of the mainland's biggest provincial and municipal mobile phone networks from its state-owned parent, the China Mobile Communications Corporation. The regions covered are Beijing, Tianjin, Shanghai, Liaoning, Hebei, Shandong and Guangxi.[16] This acquisition was backed by Vodafone, who agreed in October 2000 to invest US$ 2.5 billion to help fund the US$ 34 billion deal. With this investment, Vodafone would gain a 2.6 per cent stake in China Mobile's current US$ 96 billion market value.[17]

The MII's support of China Unicom's launch of a record US$ 5 billion initial public offering in Hong Kong and New York in June 2000 was another success of utilizing overseas capital for China's telecom development. Following China Unicom, Netcom and Jitong also revealed plans to go public in Hong Kong and other overseas markets. Meanwhile the MII has restructured the local branches of China Telecom to prepare them to be listed in Hong Kong and other overseas stock markets. It also proposed to apply the build-operate-transfer (BOT) model to encourage investment in telecom infrastructure in China's inland regions.[18] Against the downturn of the world telecom market, China Telecom moved on to launch its initial public offering for 16.8 billion shares in New York and Hong Kong in November 2002 in order to raise up to US$ 3.68 billion. The newly listed corporation has China Telecom's network assets in some of the mainland's wealthiest regions – the provinces of Guangdong, Jiangsu and Zhejiang – and the municipality of Shanghai, China's bustling financial capital. It also has a plan of buying five provincial networks from its state-run parent within six months of its initial public offering.[19]

A subtle objective of these offshore fund-raising efforts is to make it easier for these Chinese state-owned carriers to fulfil China's commitment to allow a 49 per cent for foreign shareholding upon its entry into the WTO. If every Chinese carrier had a significant portion of its assets owned by the overseas subsidiary of its state-owned parent, little would be left for the real foreign companies to snap up in the 49 per cent stake allowable for foreign ownership.

Such a strategy will maintain the state's control over the effective share of foreign ownership in the telecom business.

Setting Regulatory Rules

Signing the WTO deal binds China to the principles outlined in the *WTO Basic Telecom Agreement of 1997*, which stipulates that a member country must implement transparent regulatory framework that will:

- prevent anti-competitive practices (particularly by the dominant incumbent);
- ensure interconnection (under non-discriminatory, transparent, reasonable terms and cost-oriented rates);
- administer universal service obligations transparently and fairly;
- implement an open and fair licensing process;
- allocate telecom resources in an objective, timely, transparent and non-discriminatory manner; and
- have an independent impartial regulatory body.[20]

To meet these requirements, China first promulgated the *Telecommunications Regulations* in September 2000. The general principles of the regulations are stated as:

> to standardize the order of the telecommunications (telecom hereafter) market, safeguard the legitimate interests of both subscribers and operators of telecom services, and ensure the security of telecom networks and information so as to promote the healthy development of telecom activities in the country (Article 1).

Generally, the *Regulations* provide for the first time a regulatory framework that aims to conform to WTO requirements. There are, however, still some grey areas that need further regulatory provisions to clarify (Table 5.2). Nevertheless, the rules in the *Regulations* are long in ensuring the state control over the basic telecom network by spelling out the following rules:

1. *Licensing authority*

    All telecom businesses are classified into two types: (a) the basic telecom business operator who provides public network infrastructure, data and voice transmission services; (b) the value-adding telecom business operator who uses the public network to provide telecom and information services. All basic telecom business operators and the value-adding telecom business operators whose service scope covers two or more provincial territories must be licensed from 'the department in charge of the information industry under the State Council' (DII-SC). Other value-adding telecom business operators should be licensed by provincial telecom regulatory bodies.

2.   *State share in telecom business*
      A basic telecom business operator can only be licensed as a legally established corporation in which the state share or stake is no less than 51 per cent (the controlling stake).

3.   *State intervention in tariff/rate setting*
      Telecom tariffs/rates consist of market-coordinated prices (set by service providers), government-guided prices (that is floating ranges allowed for operators to set their prices/rates), and government-set prices (for important tariff rates). Pricing is mainly cost-based. The DII-SC is authorized to play a pivotal role in government involvement in telecom tariff/rate setting.

4.   *State role in telecom resource allocation*
      The principle of 'a pay-for-use scheme for utilization of telecom resources based on unified planning, centralized management and rational allocation' is spelled out for telecom resource allocation. Administrative assignment is a major allocating measure along with tender/auction.

5.   *State control of fixed capital investment*
      DII-SC has unified planning authority over the development of public telecom networks, specialized telecom networks and transmission networks for radio and television broadcasting. As long as these projects involve nationwide information network projects or construction projects exceeding the state-defined quota, approval must be obtained from the DII-SC before such projects can go through the state approval procedure for capital construction projects. Telecom network's design, development and operation by any player must meet the requirements and standards of national security and network security.

Table 5.2   WTO requirements versus China's regulatory framework

Requirements by WTO basic telecom agreement	Telecom Regulations (2000)	Remarks
Prevent anti-competitive practices	Spell out the prohibited anti-competitive practices in Articles 41 and 42	The principles are in line with WTO requirements

Ensure interconnection	Section 2 of Chapter Two (Articles 17–22) specifies obligations and procedures for interconnection. The principles of interconnection are 'technical feasibility, economic rationality, fairness and justice, and mutual cooperation' (Article 17)	*Measures for Interconnection between Public Networks* was promulgated in May 2001 to provide more details of the procedures
Administer universal service obligations transparently and fairly	Article 44 specifies that DII-SC can assign or tender universal service obligations to operators. The cost-compensation measures are to be worked out by DII-SC with fiscal and price authorities of State Council	There is no clear definition of this obligation. Details are yet to be provided by further provisions
Implement open and fair licensing process	Articles 10 and 13 clearly specify the qualifications for Basic Telecom Licence and Value-added Telecom Licence respectively. Article 9 specifies the licensing authorities	Details of licensing procedures are provided by *Regulations on the Licence for Operation of Telecom Business* (February 2002); Length of licence is specified as 5 or 10 years for Basic Telecom operation and 5 years for other licences.
Allocate telecom resources in an objective, timely, transparent and non-discriminatory manner	Article 27 spells out the principle of 'a pay-for-use scheme for utilization of telecom resources based on unified planning, centralized management and rational allocation' for telecom resources allocation Assignment and tender/auction are the two ways of allocating telecom resources (Article 29)	Enough room is left for administrative discretions in allocating telecom resources. The administrative assignment procedures are not clearly stipulated

Have an independent impartial regulatory body	Article 3: 'The department in charge of the information industry under the State Council is entitled to exercise supervision and regulation over the country's telecom industry in accordance with this set of regulations'	The MII was thought to be equivalent to DII-SC. Its status has been under question, however, since the State Leading Group for Informatization, a supra-ministry panel headed by Premier Zhu Rongji, was set up in September 2001[21]

5.5   SAFEGUARD FOR STATE CONTROL

To meet its commitments for joining WTO, the State Council immediately revamped the policy towards foreign direct investment in the telecom sector on the date (11 December 2001) of China's accession by promulgating the *Regulations on Foreign-invested Telecom Enterprises.*[22] On 4 March 2002, China promulgated a new *Catalogue of Industries for Guiding Foreign-funded Investment,*[23] in which the 'telecom companies' are under the 'restricted' category with the following details:

1. *Value-added telecommunications and paging in basic telecom services* From 11 December 2001, foreign investment is allowed up to 30 per cent of total assets; foreign capital share is to be allowed up to 49 per cent by 11 December 2002 and to be allowed up to 50 per cent by 11 December 2003.
2. *Mobile telephony and data transmission in basic telecommunications* From 11 December 2001, foreign investment is allowed up to 25 per cent of total assets; foreign capital share is to be allowed up to 35 per cent by 11 December 2002 and to be allowed up to 49 per cent by 11 December 2003.
3. *Domestic and international businesses of basic telecommunications* From 11 December 2001, foreign investment is allowed up to 25 per cent of total assets; foreign capital share is to be allowed up to 35 per cent by 11 December 2002 and to be allowed up to 49 per cent by 11 December 2003.

Licensing and Approval Procedures

On the same day when the State Council promulgated the *Regulations on Foreign-invested Telecom Enterprises,* the MII issued the No. 19 Ministerial Decree to promulgate the *Regulations on the License for Operation of Telecommunications Business.*[24] Both regulations took effect on 1 January 2002. Besides spelling out detail procedures of licensing, both regulations impose minimum registered capital requirements for foreign-invested as well as domestic telecom companies (Table 5.3).

Table 5.3   Minimum registered capital requirements and other licensing constraints

Geographic range of operation	Basic Telecom	Value-added services
Within a province, autonomous region or municipality	RMB 200 million/ US$ 24.15 million	RMB 1 million/ US$ 0.121 million
Nationwide or across provincial borders	RMB 2 billion/ US$ 241.55 million	RMB 10 million/ US$ 1.21 million
Maximum foreign share allowed (%)	49	50
Length of application review at DII-SC	180 days	90 days
Length of licence	5 or 10 years	5 years

Source: The MII, *Regulations on the Licence for Operation of Telecommunications Business* and *Regulations on Foreign-invested Telecom Enterprises.*

These requirements form the financial barriers for entry to the market. As a reference, before the MII transferred the Guoxin Paging Company (with assets valued at RMB 13 billion) to China Unicom, the latter had only assets worth RMB 2.3 billion (see Chapter 3), just above the RMB 2 billion minimum registered capital requirements set in these regulations.

Another noticeable requirement is that the review of application for approval is based on the qualifications of the 'major Chinese [or foreign] investor', who is defined as 'the one that makes the largest contribution among all the Chinese [or foreign] investors, which accounts for more than 30 per cent of the total contribution by all the Chinese [or foreign] investors' (Articles 8 and 9 of *Regulations on Foreign-invested Telecom Enterprises*).

A venture will thus not be approved if a qualified major investor with such a considerable stake is absent on either side. This requirement rules out the consortiums made of investors whose shares of stakes cannot reach the 30 per cent threshold. For instance, to be able to apply for a basic telecom licence, a venture with a Chinese foreign share ratio of 51:49 must have a Chinese major investor holding no less than 15.3 per cent (= 0.30×51) and a foreign major investor holding no less than 14.7 per cent (= 0.30×49) of the total capital assets.

After China's accession to WTO, the MII and the SDPC jointly promulgated the *Provisions of Telecom Network Construction*, to take effect on 1 February 2002.[25] The regulation covers the construction of public telecom network, the specialized telecom network and the radio and television transmission network (Article 2). It states the principles of the telecom network construction as to 'protect national sovereignty, eliminate monopoly, encourage competition, promote rational resource utilization, maintain orders of communications construction market, nurture open, fair and just competition environment' (Article 6).

The MII is in charge of compiling the telecom industry's national development plan while the provincial communications bureaus (PCBs) are in charge of compiling intra-provincial telecom development plans. [26] All enterprises investing in telecom network must draft five-year enterprise plans, five-year project plans and annual rolling plans for the enterprise and projects in line with the national and provincial development plans (Article 7). These enterprises must submit their five-year plans to the MII and related authorities before the starting date of every national FYP and the annual rolling plans before the end of January every year for filing (Article 12). Except for annual project plans, all the filed plans will automatically take effect if the MII and other authorities do not raise objections within 30 days after filing. The annual project plans, however, must be reviewed and approved by the MII or PCBs (Article 13).

For domestic transmission network construction or upgrading, before a project goes to the government's review-and-approval procedures for capital construction projects, it must first go through a preliminary review-and-approval process by the authorities in charge of telecommunications (Article 17). As for international transmission network and gateways, the projects above RMB 100 million or US$ 30 million (if foreign investment is involved) must be first approved by the MII before they can be submitted to the SDPC or the State Economic and Trade Commission or the State Council for approval. Projects below the threshold must be approved by the MII (Article 20).

By their design, these regulations provide safeguards for the continuity of a centrally planned regime for the construction and development of telecom infrastructure after the sector is open to foreign investors. In addition, to ensure 'national sovereignty', the government has introduced a series of regulations to protect national security in the cyberspace.

Sovereignty in Cyberspace

On 25 January 2000, China's State Secrets Bureau issued the 'State Secrecy Protection Regulations for Computer Information Systems on the Internet'. It stipulated in Article 15 that:

> National backbone networks, Internet access providers and users shall accept the supervision and inspection conducted by departments in charge of protecting secrets and shall cooperate with them. They shall assist secret-protection departments in investigating illegal actions that divulge state secrets on the Internet.[27]

Of the six chapters of the *Telecommunications Regulations of the People's Republic of China* (2000), a whole chapter is devoted to the issue of telecom security. The chapter specifies that telecom operators should design, construct and operate their telecom network completely in compliance with what is required by national security and telecom network security (Article 61).

The national security concern was accompanied by the government's urge to maintain political stability and ideological controls. Such an urge was highlighted by the fact that, along with the postal and telecom services, radio and television broadcasting stations and production of broadcasting programmes and movies were also listed under the category for 'projects prohibited to foreign investment' in the 1997 Catalogue of Industries for Guiding Foreign-funded Investment. These businesses remain in the prohibited category even in the 2002 Catalogue. As for Internet, a national firewall system effectively blocks access to hundreds of overseas websites. According to research done in early September 2002 on China's Internet censorship, sites blocked include popular search engines like Google and AltaVista, non-government organizations like Amnesty International and Human Rights Watch, as well as media websites like The New York Times, BBC News, CBS News and The Guardian.[28]

The *Telecommunications Regulations* holds a telecom operator responsible to stop the transmission of the information with any of the contents specified below and to keep the related record in custody and to send the corresponding reports to the related department of the state immediately (Article 62). Such contents (Article 57) include those that tend to:

- run counter the basic principles specified by the Constitution;
- harm the national security, leak state secrets, subvert the state political power and impede the country's unification;
- harm the state reputation and interests; instigate ethnic enmity, give rise to racial discrimination and harm national solidarity;

- break the country's religious policies, disseminate ideas of evil cults and superstitions; spread rumours to disturb the social order and stability;
- spread obscene and criminal senses; and
- insult or defame others and harm the legal interests of others.

Lukewarm Influx

Given these safeguards, it is no wonder that FDI influx in the telecom operations since China's accession to the WTO has been lukewarm. In March 2002, AT&T became the first partially foreign-owned telecom carrier to offer services in China when it officially launched telecom services in Shanghai through a joint venture with Shanghai Symphony Telecommunications. It holds a 25 per cent share in the company, with Shanghai Telecom holding 60 per cent and Shanghai Information Investment holding 15 per cent. [29] Another well-publicized foreign-invested telecom venture, Alcatel Shanghai Bell, was officially launched in Shanghai on 28 May 2002, one day prior to the convening of the APEC Ministerial Meeting of Telecommunications and Information Industry. Although Alcatel controls 50+1 per cent share in the company (according to an agreement made in October 2001), the foreign dominance in shareholding does not make a breakthrough since its business niche is mainly being a 'strong and advanced manufacturing centre'.[30]

Other cases of foreign participation are either in the value-added services or in specific network construction projects. For instance, Telstra of Australia reportedly was negotiating for a joint venture with Shanghai General Electronics Group to provide telecom services in the greater Shanghai region, in particular broadband services, with an initial stake for Telstra around 30 per cent.[31] In July 2002, Pacific Century CyberWorks formed a RMB 200 million (US$ 24 million) joint venture with China Telecom to provide IT services to the mainland financial sector. The Hong Kong company chaired by Richard Li Tzar-kai is to take 48.5 per cent share of the joint venture.[32]

One of the largest network projects with foreign participation has been the construction of a 17-city broadband network catering for commercial users, which is jointly invested by China Netcom and Paris-based global carrier Equant. The two companies announced in August 2002 the expansion of their network to cover 26 other cities by the end of 2002.[33] Other big network projects include China Unicom's CDMA network based on Binary Runtime Environment for Wireless (BREW), to be developed with Qualcomm by the end of 2002,[34] and Unicom's US$ 40-million contract with Nortel Networks to expand GSM networks in the autonomous regions of Xinjiang Uygur and Ningxia Hui, Shanxi province and Chongqing municipality.[35] In January 2003, China Unicom signed an agreement with SK Telecom, South Korea's largest mobile carrier, to establish a wireless Internet joint venture focus on CDMA 1x business in China. SK Telecom would take a 49 per cent stake in the joint venture, while China Unicom would have the remaining 51 per cent.[36]

Industrial observers offered two main reasons to explain why major foreign telecom operators did not enter into the Chinese telecom market in the first year after China's WTO accession. First, entry requires prudent planning, perfect preparation and a huge input of human resources. Second, the downturn of the world telecom industry in 2001–02 has kept the big telecom players busy with their own debt-ridden balance sheets.[37]

On top of these reasons, Gao (2002) observed that the second divestiture of China Telecom and other restructures in the domestic telecom sector increased the uncertainty for foreign players to select joint venture partners in the months after China's accession to WTO. The series of regulations introduced in these months need more explanations and their restrictive clauses have surely imposed effective constraints on foreign participation. A more competitive domestic market has also made it more difficult for foreign carriers to make a profitable entry.

From these observations, we may conclude that the Chinese government has so far in the first stage following the WTO accession been quite successful in pursuing its strategy to pre-empt foreign entrants' 'cream-skimming', to protect business interests of domestic carriers from being threatened by the entry of 'foreign wolves', and to ensure state control over basic telecom business and network development. There are, however, more challenges and unsolved issues ahead.

Summary

In the past, China's policy makers were reluctant to open up the telecom service market for foreign equity investment due to considerations of national security, sovereignty and interests of indigenous carriers. The national stakes in the WTO membership, however, overrode such industrial stakes. To prepare for post-WTO opening, the Chinese regulators have pursued a strategy to pre-empt foreign entrants 'cream-skimming' and to safeguard state control over basic telecom business and network-building.

NOTES

1. 'WTO Ministerial Conference approves China's accession', *WTO News 2001*, Press 252, 10 November 2001 (http://www.wto.org/english/news_e/pres01_e/pr252_e.htm).

2. For instance, see Wu X. 'Dancing with wolves: China's IT industry faces WTO', China News Agency, 12 November 2001 (www.people.com.cn/GB/it/48/297/20011112/603095.html).
3. *Beijing Review* (Beijing), 14–20 June 1993.
4. *China Economic News*, Beijing, 24 July 1995.
5. *China Economic News*, Beijing, 2 March 1998.
6. Reuters news, *Business Times* (Singapore), 2 December 1998.
7. *Far Eastern Economic Review* (Hong Kong), 30 September 1999.
8. Reuters news, *Business Times* (Singapore), 2 December 1998.
9. *China Daily* (Hong Kong), 17 October 1999.
10. Optus is the second largest telecom company in Australia, operating mobile, data services and multimedia. SingTel acquired Optus for A$ 14 billion in September 2001, stirring up public fears over a potential threat to Australian national security as Optus maintains a satellite that is used for defence purpose. The deal was approved only after assurance from SingTel that it would not compromise Australia's national interests. (*Radio Singapore International* (Singapore), 24 August 2001, http://www.rsi.com.sg.
11. 'China and the WTO: long march', *The Economist* (UK), 1 April 1999.
12. Jasper Becker, 'Princes of privatisation reign', *South China Morning Post*, 10 January 2002.
13. AFP's report on the EU–China deal, *Straits Times* (Singapore), 20 May 2000.
14. *China Online News*, 26 December 2000.
15. 'Telecoms – after the break up', *China Economic Review* (Janet Matthews Information Services), 11 June 2002.
16. 'China Telecom (HK) changes name to China Mobile', *China Online News*, 22 May 2000, http://www.chinaonline.com.
17. 'Vodafone buys into China Mobile', *Straits Times* (Singapore), 5 October 2000.
18. Interview with officials and scholars of Shanghai Institute of P & T Economy, 8 July 2000.
19. 'China Telecom mulls network purchase', *Financial Times* (FT.com), 24 October 2002; 'China Telecom's IPO', *China Communications News* (www.c114.net/news/), 25 October 2002.
20. 'Background note on the WTO negotiations on basic telecommunications', *WTO Press Release*, 22 February 1996.
21. *China Daily* (New York), 26 September 2001.
22. Ministry of Information Industry website, http://www.mii.gov.cn/mii/hyzw/hygl.html.
23. Ministry of Foreign Trade and Economic Co-operation website, http://www.moftec.gov.cn /flfgqd.shtml.

24. Ministry of Information Industry website,
http://www.mii.gov.cn/mii/hyzw/hygl.html.

25. Ministry of Information Industry website,
http://www.mii.gov.cn/mii/zcfg.html.

26. China's 10th Five-year Plan covers the period 2001–005. The MII
promulgated *Highlights of Information Industry's 10th Five-year Plan*
in May 2001 (http://www.chinaccia.org.cn).

27. *China Online News*, 26 January 2000, http://www.chinaonline.com.

28. AFP, 'Harvard student finds China blocks hundreds of websites',
Business Times (Singapore), 9 September 2002.

29. 'AT&T launches China services, first foreign telecom JV', *Asiainfo
Daily China News* (28 March 2002).

30. 'China's first foreign-invested telecom firm launched in Shanghai',
Xinhua News Agency (28 May 2002).

31. 'Telstra says in negotiations on venture with Shanghai Sydney', *AAP
Newsfeed* (2 July 2002).

32. 'Finance foray for CyberWorks, China Telecom; Partners eye piece of
US$7b IT spending pie', *South China Morning Post* (12 July 2002).

33. 'Alliance expands China plans; Equant–CNC venture accelerates
roll-out schedule after 35 per cent growth in customer connections',
South China Morning Post (21 August 2002).

34. 'China Unicom selects Qualcomm's BREW solution as its platform to
launch wireless data applications', *PR Newswire* (26 August 2002).

35. 'Nortel Networks wins US$40 million in China Unicom expansion
contracts; adding capacity for 925,000 new subscribers, creating
platform for wireless data', *Business Wire* (23 September 2002).

36. 'SK Telecom signs joint venture deal with China Unicom', Global
Wireless.com, 17 January 2003.

37. 'Telecom industry developing trends in China', *Asiainfo Daily China
News* (19 July 2002).

6. New developments and prospects

In the first six months after China became a member of the World Trade Organization (WTO), the country's telecom sector experienced another drastic overhaul: China Telecom, the nation's fixed-line monopoly, which accounted for over 50 per cent of the country's telecom revenue in 2001, was transversely cut into two parts along regional lines. This second divestiture of China Telecom was decided by the State Council before China sealed its WTO entry deal in November 2001 and was finally consummated in May 2002 with the launch of two new telecom operators, namely, the (new) China Telecom Corporation and the China Netcom Communications Group Corporation.

The latter, a merger between the former Netcom and Jitong, took over the former China Telecom's network assets in ten provinces in north China while the reborn China Telecom inherited the rest. With the birth of these two new fixed-line giant carriers, the nation's telecom market has become the competing ground of a total of six players, including China Unicom, China Mobile, China Satcom (launched by end of 2001) and Railcom (launched in January 2001). Some Chinese media described the event as the beginning of an era of 'Warring States' in the telecom market.[1]

6.1   THE SECOND DIVESTITURE

The former China Telecom Group was vertically divested in early 2000 along business functional lines. As discussed in Chapter 3, the Ministry of Information Industry (MII) won the State Council's approval of its 'vertical divestiture' plan after carefully comparing the plan's pros and cons against the alternative 'horizontal divestiture' plan suggested by some scholars. It thus came as a surprise to many that less than two years after the first divestiture, China Telecom, the fixed-line network operator, which resulted from the first divestiture, should be further divided into two companies by regional lines.

The Second-tier Interest Groups

In contrast to the former Ministry of Post and Telecommunications (MPT)-affiliated 'first-tier interests', the late entrants in the telecom market were dubbed as the 'second-tier interest groups' by scholars such as Han Deqiang, a professor at the Beijing University of Aeronautics and Astronautics (Wan, 2001). In China, the second divestiture of China Telecom was widely believed to be a conspiracy of the 'second-tier interest groups'.

Table 6.1   Market shares of major carriers (2001)

	China Telecom	China Mobile	Unicom	Railcom	Netcom	Satcom	Jitong
Telecom total turnover (RMB 100 m)	1816.0	1616.3	N/A	37.1	N/A	N/A	N/A
Telecom revenue (RMB 100 m)	1810.0	1346.8	379.8	36.9	9.05	3.1	5.7
Share (%)	50.40	37.50	10.58	1.03	0.25	0.09	0.16
Assets (RMB 100 m)	Above 4000*	3274	1862	108	N/A	N/A	N/A
Labour productivity (RMB 10,000)	51.8	155.6	74.2	N/A	34	N/A	N/A

Note: * Figure is estimated by the authors according to earlier reports.

Source: Ministry of Information Industry, 'Statistical Communique of Tele- communications Development 2001', http://www.mii.gov.cn.

Such speculations are not unfounded. Despite its heavy investment in broadband assets, by 2001 Netcom was still a relatively small potato, in terms of business revenues, as compared to other players (Table 6.1). It was also reported to have suffered heavy business losses due to the huge expense on investment and the little revenue it could generate (Wan, 2001). It would be years before Netcom could grow up and become a powerful rival to the incumbent China Telecom. Related uncertainties for the future of Netcom included China's imminent accession to the WTO by the end of 2001 and President Jiang Zemin's expected retirement at the Communist Party's 16th National Congress in late 2002. In a post-WTO telecom market opened for foreign equity investment, Netcom would not enjoy much advantage over its rivals in utilizing foreign capital. With Jiang Zemin phasing out of the political arena, Netcom's political clout would also diminish. To Netcom, there was therefore a sense of urgency to make a decisive leap to capture a strategic height in the telecom sector before all that happened. With this perspective, it is not too difficult to comprehend the motive for the company to embark on a mission seemingly impossible for a start-up: to take over a major share of the assets of the dominant incumbent, China Telecom, by splitting up the giant.

Circumventing the MII

A few weeks before the first report of the second divestiture of China Telecom appeared in the Chinese media, the State Council made an unusual move in September 2001 to restructure the regulatory authority of the info-communications industry by setting up the State Leading Group for Informatization (SLGI). Headed by Premier Zhu Rongji, the SLGI is a supra-ministry panel including Vice-President Hu Jintao (the expected successor to President Jiang Zemin), Vice-Premier Li Lanqing, and ministers of the ministries and administrations under the State Council. Meanwhile, the National Informatization Promotion Office, a special office that directly reports to the State Council, was set up to implement the central government's policies and measures in the drive for informatization. Zeng Peiyan, the Minister of State Development and Planning Commission (SDPC), was assigned as Director-General of the new office.[2]

This organizational restructure was observed by many as an obvious step to circumvent the MII's regulatory power. By setting up a cabinet-level panel chaired by the Premier himself, Zhu Rongji had in effect withdrawn the mandate of Wu Jichuan, the Minister of Information Industry, and took over the decision making on the industry's restructuring, observed by London-based *The Economist*.[3] Compared to the former Joint Conference on State Economic Informatization/National Information Infrastructure Steering Committee (JCSEI/NIISC) task force that existed before the cabinet reshuffle at the 9th National People's Congress, this relaunched super-ministerial panel is headed by higher-ranked officials with more dominant authority over the ministries.

The Puzzling Divestiture

Shortly after the organizational change in the State Council, the report about the decision on China Telecom's second divestiture emerged in China's state-controlled press. Signs indicate that the decision was made by a top-down manner, pushed by interest groups but little consultation was made to MII officials or industrial specialists during the process.

Preparation for China Telecom's overseas listing was well on track to launch the initial public offering (IPO) in 2001. The process was suddenly halted by the State Council in January 2001. On 11 May 2001, the State Council's Office of Economic Restructuring and the SDPC arranged an emergency meeting with industrial experts to discuss the divestiture of China Telecom. Expecting a consultative hearing, these experts came to the meeting in Beijing on the next day only to find that the decision on the second divestiture had already been made. A 'horizontal divestiture' plan proposed by Merrill Lynch to divide the carrier into a north and a south part was ready for adoption. The other 'vertical divestiture' plan proposed by Morgan Stanley was also tabled (Wan, 2001).

Among Chinese experts and scholars, the majority of views were against the divestiture by regional lines. Wang Xiaoqiang, a well-known industrial economist, pointed out that effective competition should promote growth of the telecom industry. The government should not 'create competition for the sake of competition'. He considered the US AT&T divestiture in the early 1980s a wrong model to follow since the post-divestiture 'baby Bells' became regional monopolies that continued to block entry. Wang advocated setting up a network management company that specialized in network development, which would lease circuits and sell access at regulated low prices to various carriers.[4] Han Kaili, a professor at the Beijing Post and Telecom University, proposed that China Telecom should be divided into local, long-distance and data service providers rather than along regional lines (Wan, 2001).

Another economist, Zhou Qiren, an outspoken critic of monopoly structure of the telecom market in earlier years, warned against 'ineffective divestiture' that would lead to regional monopolies. He suggested that competition could be introduced by allowing mutual entries to the market segments currently under the domains of different government departments. With such entry liberalization, a further divestiture of China Telecom would not be necessary (Zhou, 2001).

Gao (2001) argued that the divestiture proposal went against merger and acquisition trends in the world telecom market. He pointed out that the monopoly problem in China mainly arose from a rigid division of business lines among different players. Cutting up China Telecom's backbone network by region would not solve such monopoly problems but would make the network operation less efficient. The second divestiture plan was 'bizarre in theory and harmful in practice'.

Despite strong opposition from experts and scholars, the 'second-tier interest groups', backed by powerful government ministries and departments and led by Netcom, were all pushing for a second divestiture for China Telecom, apparently driven by the anticipated gains from the demise of the giant.

On the other hand, China Telecom, knowing that the fate of divestiture was inevitable, 'volunteered' for the north–south division plan with the support of the MII. For China Telecom, a north–south split would minimize the damage to its business as it hoped to survive as a twin of 'North China Telecom' and 'South China Telecom', reserving monopoly on a divided national network (Wan, 2001). It, however, might not have expected that the whole network asset of the proposed 'North China Telecom' would be taken over by Netcom, a much smaller start-up.

Setting up the SLGI in September 2001 hastened the decision making over the divestiture. It is interesting to note that, according to a report by *The Economist*, the process to break up China Telecom into a northern and a southern part:

> continued with expressions of surprise by China's telecoms regulator (i.e. MII), who favoured a different plan but had not been consulted. Next, the State Council, China's cabinet, denied that any decision was final. This in turn was ignored by Beijing's elite, which was already speculating about who would get what job in the new corporate giants.[5]

The *South China Morning Post* reported that President Jiang Zemin was directly involved in the decision process. The year 2001:

> saw him strengthen his grip on this key sector and smash the deep-rooted bureaucratic opposition to privatisation led by Minister of Information Industry Wu Jichuan. Mr Wu fought tooth and nail to stop President Jiang from breaking up China Telecom and throwing the protected industry open to foreign investment. He even threatened to resign if China allowed foreigners to own up to 49 per cent of telecom companies under the World Trade Organisation deal. (Becker, 2002)

The fate of China Telecom was sealed at a State Council meeting on 12 October 2001 (Wan, 2001). China Telecom was to be divided up into two carriers. The network of 10 provincial regions in north China was to be taken over by Netcom and restructured to China Netcom Corporation Limited (CNC). The remaining network of 21 provincial regions in south China was to be retained by the new China Telecom. On top of that, Jitong would also be merged into CNC. CNC thus was the largest winner of this divestiture and Jiang Mianheng, dubbed as 'China's digital princeling', was perceived by some as a crucial figure behind the scene. 'To placate the vested bureaucratic interests, the management of the new company is to be drawn from China Telecom, not the youngsters who ran Netcom; but insiders say Mianheng is bound to remain in charge' (Becker, 2002).

6.2 UNSOLVED ISSUES

On 16 May 2002, a restructured China Telecom and China Netcom were officially launched in Beijing under their new names of 'China Telecom Corporation' and 'China Netcom Communication Group Corporation', respectively. The new China Telecom Corporation is entitled to retain the goodwill and intangible assets of 'China Telecom'. It maintains business in 21 provincial regions in southern and north-western China and holds 70 per cent of the national trunk line transmission network assets owned by the former China Telecom. The ten provincial corporations of the former China Telecom in the provinces of Beijing, Tianjin, Hebei, Henan, Shandong, Shanxi, Inner Mongolia, Heilongjiang, Jilin and Laioning, together with the former China Netcom, and Jitong Communications Corporation, were merged into the new China Netcom Communication Group Corporation (CNC), which holds 30 per cent of the national trunk line transmission network assets (Figure 6.1). Both new corporations are fixed-line telephone operators, who own the complete domestic long-distance trunk transmission networks as well as local telephone networks in their domain areas.[6]

A few months earlier, China Satellite Communications Corporation (China Satcom) was officially set up in December 2001. The corporation is based on the merging of several satellite-based telecom companies, such as China Telecommunications Broadcast Satellite Corporation, China Orient Telecom Satellite Company Limited, China Space Mobile Satellite Telecommunications Company Limited and ChinaSat of China Telecom (Hong Kong). The telecom carrier plans to provide a general network service, broadband access service, IP basic service and IP value-added service in one or two years. The corporation is capable of providing multiple information services to less-developed mountain and desert regions through satellite-based technology.[7]

With these developments, the telecom market is now shared by six corporations, namely China Telecom Corporation, China Netcom Communication Group Corporation, China Mobile, China Unicom, China Satcom and China Railcom (Table 6.2). CNC, with the combined assets of northern part of former China Telecom, old Netcom, and Jitong, jumped ahead to become the third largest player in the telecom market. The post-second-divestiture China Telecom is no longer number one in terms of revenue. The landscape of the country's telecom market has since drastically changed (Figure 6.2). Chinese media hailed the arrival of an era of 'Warring States' in China's telecom market.

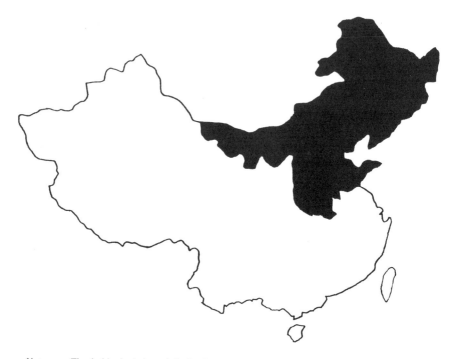

Note: The darkly shaded area is in the domain of the CNC while the lightly shaded area is in the domain of the new China Telecom.

Figure 6.1   Geographic scope of the new China Telecom and CNC

There are still several major issues unsolved in the industry's regulatory framework. First, the powerful mandate of SLGI once raised the hope for a Chinese version of 'Federal Communications Commission', which can eventually become an effective regulator for communications network development and an impartial umpire for keeping a level playing field for all powerful players backed by different governmental departments. Despite such speculations, the Ministry of Information Industry (MII) survived the administrative restructure at the 10th National People's Congress held in March 2003. Wang Xudong, an official with no post–telecom business administration background, was appointed the new minister at the Congress.

Notwithstanding this apparent step to boost the ministry as a neutral regulator, the MII may still face challenges from other ministries and government departments as it remains a ministry under the State Council. One of the immediate issues is that the cable television network under SARFT continues to stay outside the MII's regulation. For the telecom industry, the status of the future regulator has to be defined by a *Telecommunications Law*, which is yet to be adopted by legislation after being drafted for years. In the absence of the regulatory authority backed by such a law, the MII's decisions may easily be over-ruled by a supra-ministry ad hoc taskforce such as SLGI, as happened in the past. In fact, the SLGI continues to operate and dominate decision makings regarding the telecom industry.[8]

Table 6.2   Business scopes of six major carriers (after May 2002)

	China Telecom	China Mobile	Unicom	Railcom	CNC	Satcom
Local fixed line	Y		Y*	Y	Y	
Long distance	Y			Y	Y	
Backbone network	Y	Y	Y	Y	Y	Y
IP telephony	Y		Y	Y	Y	Y
Internet access	Y		Y	Y	Y	Y
Mobile telephony		Y	Y			

* with geographic restrictions to a few cities.

Second, the MII continues to play a double role of a state asset custodian in the industry as well as a consumer welfare guardian. This double-role playing has led to policy dilemmas. In fact, the MII's role as a state asset custodian often dominates its other role as a consumer welfare guardian. For instance, rather than acting as a consumer protector that keeps price ceilings on telecom rates, the MII has maintained price floors to limit ranges of rate-cutting competition between rival carriers. In the name of 'policing the market order', it has also taken great efforts to maintain the two-way fee charging structure for both the calling party and the receiving party in the mobile telephone market. The two mobile communications carriers, China Unicom and China Mobile, however, have provided various 'quasi-one-way fee' packages to customers in their battles for market shares. The two-way fee charging structure has also inadvertently created a niche for the fixed-line carriers' PHS services that offer users with one-way calling rates. Despite the MII's intervention, price wars in the mobile communications market intensified in the year after China Telecom's second divestiture (see Appendix 1). As shown in Chapter 4, the MII's paternalist concerns over the state-owned telecom carriers' revenue has not only gone against the regulator's duty to enhance consumer welfare through promoting competition, but has also failed to reconcile the conflicting interests of these giant carriers under its care.

Total revenue RMB 359 billion (2001)

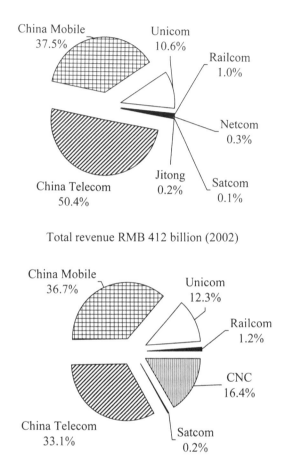

Total revenue RMB 412 billion (2002)

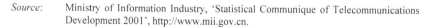

Source: Ministry of Information Industry, 'Statistical Communique of Telecommunications
              Development 2001', http://www.mii.gov.cn.

*Figure 6.2   Telecom revenue shares before and after China Telecom's
                 second divestiture (2001, 2002)*

Another glaring case of such policy dilemmas is the MII's decision to
implement an eightfold increase in the rates charged to foreign carriers for

terminating telephone calls into China on the eve of China Telecom's initial public offering in Hong Kong and New York stock markets in November 2002. Despite this last-minute bid to make the fixed-line carrier's business look more attractive, shares of China Telecom met tepid demand in their debut day, even after the size of the company's initial public offering was cut twice in the proceeding days to entice buyers.[9] Meanwhile the MII-mandated eightfold rate hike, from 2 cents per minute to 17 cents per minute, immediately caused huge price increase for telephone calls to China, leading to widespread complaints and protests, especially among Hong Kong residents and overseas Chinese. The drastic rate hike was conceived by many as 'unjustified', as the adjusted rate appeared to be higher than any operator in any other major country to terminate a call from outside the country.[10] This would consequently reduce traffic volume and might wipe out the revenue gains from the rate hike. Even China's Premier Zhu Rongji criticized the MII for being 'ignorant of the market economy' in this 'inappropriate intervention'.[11] Under mounting pressures, the MII had to scrap the hike quietly a few weeks later.

Third, the MII's double-role playing and its ill-defined regulatory status have complicated the issue of interconnection and access charges. China's *Telecommunications Regulations* specify that interconnection between different networks should follow the principles of feasibility, economic rationale, justice and fairness and mutual cooperation. The *Regulations* also make it compulsory for the dominant telecom operator to provide interconnections. However, so far the regulatory principle for deciding access charges remains absent or dubious. Economics of telecommunications tells us that, under compulsory interconnection, if the access charges to the existing local networks are set too high, redundant facility investment in such networks will be encouraged to bypass the existing network. Contrarily, if the charges are set too low, inefficient entry may occur as a consequence or the operator that owns the network will try to breach the interconnection obligations.

In China's case, the existing interconnection charges appear to have been set too low by the MII. For instance, in 2002, access charges accounted for 3.6 per cent of total revenue for China Telecom and 3.3 per cent for CNC. In comparison, access charges usually account for 15 to 30 per cent of the dominant operators' revenue in other countries. Local loop access charge in China is RMB 0.06 (about US$ 0.0073) per minute, considerably lower than the US$ 0.0157 per minute in US, the US$ 0.0237 in Japan, and the US$ 0.026 in Mexico.[12] On top of that, the two mobile telephone carriers, China Mobile and China Unicom, have a mutual-access-charge waiver agreement between them.[13]

It is interesting to note that, despite the low access charges for fixed-line public network, the MII lamented widespread wasteful facility investment in telecom networks.[14] This is largely due to the fact that, given the low access charges, the fixed-line operators are reluctant to provide good-quality interconnections for other carriers. Since the fixed-line operators themselves are barred from providing mobile telephone services, for every interconnected local mobile telephone call, the fixed-line operator only gets 20 per cent of the revenue generated. Meanwhile, many specialized networks owned by different government departments and state-owned companies are beyond the interconnection regulations and are only willing to sell access at much higher prices. The competing carriers thus have incentives to over-invest in building redundant network facilities. As for the two mobile telephone carriers, the mutual waiver of access charges eliminates incentives to provide interconnection.

This situation has led to fragmentation of China's telecom network and made it very difficult to enforce interconnection. For instance, according to tests done by Guandong Telecom Administration in April 2002 on IP telephone services, while the call-success rate for China Telecom was over 75 per cent during the peak hours, the rate for China Unicom was only 10 per cent. Most non-China-Telecom carriers also suffered from low call-success rates. Unicom thus accused China Telecom of systematically blocking interconnection and jamming lines of its rival carriers. In Henan Province, in the months after China Unicom launched its CDMA mobile telephone service in June 2002, serious interconnection problems arose between Unicom's CDMA network and China Mobile's GSM network. Success rate for calls between the two networks soon dropped to less than 10 per cent.[15] Poor interconnection and competition between networks even led to sabotage of rivals' facilities. For example, in Suining County of Sichuan Province, Unicom's communication cable was severed by its rival carrier in 2002.[16] Blockage of interconnection and sabotage of rivals' network must have become rampant so that the MII set up a taskforce with China's Supreme Court in March 2003 to look into the legal aspects of the issue and vowed to penalize the saboteurs by law.[17]

In early 2003, the MII organized a team of experts to study the settlement rates of interconnection. The team was led by Zhang Xizhu of China Academy of Social Sciences and Jerry A. Hausman of Massachusetts Institute of Technology. To isolate influences of industrial interests, the MII even excluded its own telecom research institute and the Beijing Post and Telecom University from the project.[18] The whole issue of interconnection, however, may go beyond economics. As pointed out by Shi Wei, a researcher of the State Council, since the assets of major telecom carriers and communications networks belong to various government departments, it is difficult for the MII to enforce rules of interconnections and implement the restructured access charges.[19] Even under the existing fee structure, expense on access charge was already equivalent to 24 per cent and 47 per cent respectively of Unicom and China Mobile's net profits in 2001. As a custodian of state assets of these carriers, the MII has to 'rationalize' the access charges under the pressure of various interest groups behind these carriers.

Fourth, the division of business scopes of the six carriers (see Table 6.2) reflects the feature of 'asymmetric regulation' in this industry. These restrictions on business scopes have nurtured vested interests and increasingly become barriers to mutual entry between operators of different businesses.

In practice, the major carriers have tried to break these barriers by various tricks and strategies. Providing PHS (*Xiao Ling Tong*), a quasi-mobile telephony service, proves to be an effective strategy employed by the fixed-line carriers to make a detour to enter the mobile communication market. Interestingly, China Mobile and China Unicom also tried to bypass regulatory barriers to enter the fixed-line telephone market by launching the so-called '*Wu Xian Tong* (wireless desk telephone)' in May 2003.[20] The wireless desk telephone set looks like a normal fixed-line telephone with the mobile telephone structure inside and its service is provided through the GSM network. The selling point of this service is easy installation and the lower-than- normal mobile call rates. As discussed earlier, PHS is considered by many an outdated or transitional technology. Had China Telecom got a mobile service licence, it would not have developed PHS. The wireless desk telephone is no more than a mobile telephone in disguise. It would not be a rational business choice if the mobile carriers had been allowed to enter the fixed-line business or to adjust their mobile service rates more flexibly.

A similar regulation-induced business is the controversial call- forwarding service launched by Guangdong Telecom, a provincial subsidiary of China Telecom, in several cities in January 2003.[21] This service was launched under a colourful name of *Youzi Guijia* (which literally means 'return of a roaming kid'). With this service, a mobile telephone user at home can avoid paying the receiving-party fee or the call-forwarding fee, which the mobile operator would charge, by placing the mobile telephone on a gadget which forwards the call to the user's fixed-line telephone. By offering such a service, Guangdong Telecom virtually 'steals' the revenue from the mobile carriers.

In the near future, an interesting policy option to watch will be the procedure of issuing more new mobile phone licences. It is likely that one or more mobile licences will be available pretty soon. It will be a testing ground for the new regulatory regime to watch whether these licences will be auctioned off in an open and transparent process or simply be given away to whoever is politically more powerful. As a related issue, once the fixed-line carriers are allowed to operate mobile services, the interconnection arrangement will be crucial to ensure a level playing field between the rival players.

Mutual entry is also an issue between CNC and the (new) China Telecom, the two fixed-line carriers arising from the second divestiture of China Telecom. After the divestiture, CNC and China Telecom lost no time to enter each others' markets. By mid 2003, both had set up branches in almost all provinces in each others' territories. These branches in the rival's territory typically have to rely on their counterparts to get access to the local fixed-line network. Blessed by the MII, the two companies signed agreements on 'network resource cooperation' and 'interconnection arrangements between branch companies in several provinces' in December 2002.[22]These inter- connection arrangements were put into practice by mid-2003 between their local branches.

An interesting mutual entry case to watch is the possible removal of barriers between telecom businesses under the MII regulation and the cable television services under the administration of SARFT. Given Netcom's plan to purchase local cable television networks in the past, it remains to be seen whether the CNC will break the ice by being allowed to enter into the cable television market.

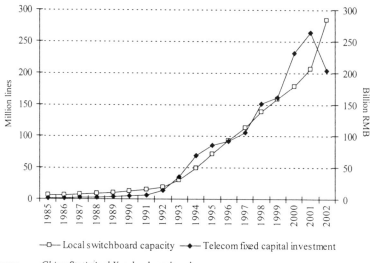

Source: *China Statistical Yearbook*, various issues.

Figure 6.3   Investment-propelled network expansion

Last but not least, who will be responsible for the provision of universal service in an increasingly competitive market? In the past two decades, the fast expansion of the telecom network has been supported by fast-growing investment (Figure 6.3). With the overhaul of the telecom market, operators have grown more cautious about investment returns. Thanks to deeper penetration of telecom usage, major telecom operators have seen their average revenue per user (ARPU) declining despite the growing number of users recently.

Table 6.3   Per capita GDP, fixed-line and mobile penetration rates (2000)

Region	Nominal GDP per capita (US$)	GDP index	Fixed-line penetration rate (%)	FLPR index	Mobile phone penetration rate (%)	MPPR index
National	841	1.00	11.44	1.00	6.74	1.00
Shanghai	3,284	3.90	32.80	2.87	21.45	3.18
Beijing	2,166	2.58	31.84	2.78	24.89	3.69
Tianjin	1,978	2.35	24.68	2.16	12.29	1.82
Zhejiang	1,559	1.85	18.90	1.65	14.39	2.14
Jiangsu	1,394	1.66	15.30	1.34	8.3	1.23
Fujian	1,364	1.62	16.22	1.42	12.47	1.85
Guangdong	1,350	1.61	16.37	1.43	15.48	2.30
Liaoning	1,331	1.58	16.52	1.44	11.59	1.72
Shandong	1,136	1.35	12.18	1.06	5.45	0.81
Heilongjiang	1,065	1.27	13.20	1.15	9.16	1.36
Hebei	911	1.08	9.89	0.86	4.77	0.71
Hubei	857	1.02	9.06	0.79	3.73	0.55
Xinjiang	856	1.02	9.92	0.87	3.84	0.57
Jilin	806	0.96	13.16	1.15	7.44	1.10
Hainan	796	0.95	8.77	0.77	7.37	1.09
Inner Mongolia	712	0.85	8.71	0.76	4.84	0.72
Hunan	692	0.82	9.91	0.87	3.91	0.58
Henan	670	0.80	9.85	0.86	3.3	0.49
Chongqing	621	0.74	8.71	0.76	5.08	0.75
Qinghai	614	0.73	7.14	0.62	3.86	0.57
Anhui	613	0.73	8.09	0.71	3.46	0.51
Shanxi	602	0.72	9.19	0.80	4.52	0.67

Jiangxi	584	0.69	8.55	0.75	3.43	0.51
Sichuan	582	0.69	6.74	0.59	4.03	0.60
Ningxia	571	0.68	10.68	0.93	5.52	0.82
Shaanxi	556	0.66	9.57	0.84	4.22	0.63
Guangxi	552	0.66	7.11	0.62	3.68	0.55
Yunnan	551	0.66	6.74	0.59	4.52	0.67
Tibet	542	0.64	4.20	0.37	2.29	0.34
Gansu	464	0.55	7.03	0.61	2.46	0.36
Guizhou	340	0.40	4.37	0.38	2.24	0.33

Source: *China Statistical Yearbook 2001* and *Yearbook of China Transportation and Communications 2001.*

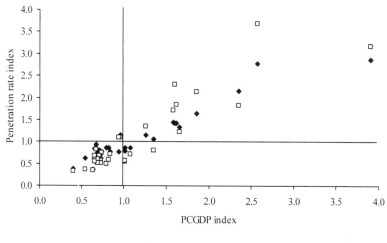

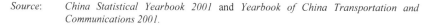

Source: *China Statistical Yearbook, 2001* and *Yearbook of China Transportation and Communications, 2001.*

Figure 6.4   Inter-regional digital gap versus income gap (2000)

If more competition is to be introduced, the telecom carriers will be increasingly concerned about profitability and become less growth-oriented. After becoming public-listed companies in overseas markets, major telecom carriers must reveal earnings and expenses following acceptable accounting rules. Their obligations to provide universal service, if not properly spelled out, will either be a risk factor for investors or be pushed aside by profit pursuing.

In China's rapidly growing economy, the inter-regional digital gap is even bigger than the income gap. As shown in Table 6.3 and Figure 6.4, by the end of 2000, there were 13 provincial regions that had per capita income above the national average. There were 11 provincial regions with a fixed-line telephone penetration rate or a mobile phone penetration rate above the national level. Most of the 31 regions were below the national average in terms of telecom penetration rate. It still has a long way to go to achieve a universal service.

The growing competition will probably stimulate telecom carriers to concentrate their investment in the eastern and urban areas where the returns are higher. This would have a negative impact on investment in network construction in the less-developed areas and, therefore, undermine the principle of universal service provision. In January 2002, the MII proposed setting up a universal service fund. Under such a fund, all telecom companies must offer universal services, guaranteeing the coordinated development of networks in central and western China as well as in rural areas.[23] The details of the fund, however, are yet to be worked out.

6.3 PROSPECTS

China's industrial policy makers want to promote the information technology (IT) industry as the 'foundation, pioneer, and pillar' of the Chinese economy in the 21st century. 'Speeding up the informatization of the national economy' is high on the agenda of China's 10th Five-year Plan (2001–05). To the Chinese leadership, the possibility of using IT to accelerate China's industrialization is an opportunity in the new century for China to catch up with the West (Zhu, 2000). As the engine and backbone of the IT industry, the telecom sector will surely continue to play a strategic role in the government's industrial policy.

According to the 10th Five-year Plan (2001–05) drafted by the MII,[24] the IT industry continues to be 'a pillar industry' in the national economy. During the 10th Five-year Plan period, the information industry will continue to grow at a rate of three times the rate of growth of the national economy. In 2005, the value added of the IT industry will account for more than 7 per cent of the gross domestic product (GDP) of which telecom will account for 4.7 per cent, and electronic products will account for 2.5 per cent. The telecom network is perceived to be the infrastructure of the national economy while network and information security is viewed as an important area in national security.

The rate of growth in the communications industry will continue to outstrip the overall economic growth rate. Revenue from the communications industry will amount to RMB 1 trillion (based on an average yearly growth rate of 23.38

per cent), of which revenue generated by the telecom network will account for RMB 920 billion, three times that of year 2000.

For communications capacity, optical cable will reach 2.5 million km in length (over 500,000 km for long-distance cabling) and cover nearly all the cities and villages in the whole country. Fixed telephone capacity will reach 300 million and total wireless network capacity will reach 360 million subscribers. The number of telephone subscribers will reach 500 million, achieving a penetration rate of over 40 per cent. Telephone connection will be provided in 95 per cent of the administrative villages.

Fixed telephone subscribers will reach 240–280 million, accounting for 20 per cent of the world total. Main-line penetration will increase from 11 per cent in 2000 to 18 per cent, exceeding the world average of 17.65 per cent. The number of mobile subscribers will reach 260–290 million, accounting for one-quarter of the world total. The penetration rate will increase from 6.7 per cent to 21 per cent, exceeding the world average of 15 per cent. Data, multimedia and Internet subscribers will reach 200 million (a 15 per cent penetration rate). With countrywide coverage by radio broadcasting and television networks, cable television subscribers will reach 150 million.

To fulfil these goals, investment in the whole IT industry will reach RMB 1700 billion during the 10th Five-year Plan period of which the telecom sector and the IT manufacturing sector will account for RMB 1250 billion and 400 billion, respectively. The investment output ratio for the telecom industry will increase from 1:1.5 in year 2000 to 1:3.3 in 2005.

Whether China will achieve these grand goals for info-communications development largely depends on how soon and how well its regulatory framework adapts to the new era of competition. In this new era, the state-owned domestic carriers, joined by their foreign partners, will play a sophisticated game in an increasingly competitive market.

As the discourse of this book has shown, in the past, business interests have been closely intertwined with political influences. The effectiveness of a regulatory regime has always been dependent on a subtle balance of political-economic interests. Power turfs have been a norm of life. Seemingly officially sanctioned rules and institutions have often ended up with unexpected twists and turns in practice.

Since the country's accession to the WTO, business practice as well as regulatory supervision has become increasingly rule-based and is gradually converging to a common international practice. Notwithstanding that, it would be naïve to expect old habits and influences to die out soon and easily. Meanwhile, the telecommunications development in this huge nation will continue to display its distinct 'Chinese characteristics'. For potential entrants who are peeping into this market of great potential, this book may offer some useful insights and tips.

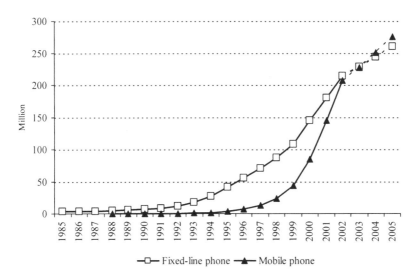

Figure 6.5   *Growth of China's telephone users (1985–2005)*

NOTES

1. The 'Warring States' (475–221 BC) was a period full of wars and conflicts among seven major states in China's history.
2. 'State to launch specific information industry unit', *China Daily* (overseas edition, New York), 26 September 2001.
3. 'China Telecom: into the crucible', *The Economist* (UK), 1 November 2001.
4. '*Fenchai youshui bu da* (Divestiture is not worth while: experts' views)', *IT Jingli Shijie* (*IT Managers' World*, China), 11 July 2001.
5. 'China Telecom: into the crucible', *The Economist* (UK), 1 November 2001.
6. Xinhua Economic News Service, 17 May 2002.

7.   'China sets up another telecom giant', Ministry of Foreign Trade and
      Economic Cooperation, (www.moftec.gov.cn), 20 December 2001.
8.   The SLGI after the the 10th National People's Congress is headed by
      Wen Jiabao, the new Premier. The deputy heads are Huang Ju, Liu
      Yunshan, Zeng Peiyan, and Zhou Yongkang.
9.   'China Telecom IPO sours', *CNN News*, http://money.cnn.com/
      2002/11/14/markets/ipo/china_telecom/
10.   'China Telecom Rate Hike', *New Telephony*, 6 November 2002, 1 (26),
      http://www.newtelephony.com.
11.   *Lianhe Zaobao* (*United Mornings*, Singapore), 20 November 2002.
12.   'Low interconnection charges: a barrier to telecom development',
      China Communications Net, http://www.c114.net, 24 February 2003.
13.   The two mobile telephone carriers waive the interconnection charges
      between them because the two-way fee structure for mobile
      communications makes such interconnection charges unnecessary.
14.   'Wu Jichuan's farewell speech', China Communications Net,
      http://www.c114.net, 24 February 2003.
15.   'China's telecom market: the painful interconnection', China
      Communications Net, http://www.c114.net, 19 December 2002.
16.   Ibid.
17.   'MII seeks criminal charges against saboteurs of interconnection',
      China Communications Net, http://www.c114.net, 3 April 2003.
18.   'Interconnection arrangements: MII redesigns interconnection
      settlement rates', China Communications Net, http://www.c114.net, 17
      March 2003.
19.   Ibid.
20.   'Xiao Ling Tong vs. Wu Xian Tong', China Communications Net,
      http://www.c114.net, 20 June 2003.
21.   'China Telecom launches controversial mobile call-forwarding service',
      Global Wireless.com, 3 January 2003.
22.   'China Telecom and CNC interconnected in most provinces', China
      Communications Net, http://www.c114.net, 19 December 2002.
23.   'Telecom sector needs a universal service fund, official says', *China
      Online News*, 30 January 2002.
24.   'China: Summary of the Tenth Five-year Plan (2001–2005) –
      Information Industry', Telecommunications Research Project,
      University of Hong Kong, www.trp.hku.hk.

Appendix 1. Main events of China's telecommunications sector (1979–2003)

Date	Event
1979	The State Council made the Ministry of Post and Telecommunications (MPT) the dominant central planner of nationwide postal and telecom developments. Local post and telecom enterprises (PTEs) were put under the 'dual leadership' of provincial governments and the MPT.
1980	The State Council adopted a policy of developing a local (intra-city) telephone service with local (intra-city) telephone revenues. Local PTEs: • gained full control over the local (intra-city) telephone service revenues; • were authorized to charge phone subscribers expensive installation fees, ranging between RMB 1,000 to RMB 2,000 per terminal for commercial phone lines and between RMB 300 to RMB 500 for residential users.
October 1984	The State Council stipulated a 'six-point instruction' to give priority to postal and telecom development, giving a green light to upward adjustment of telecom service rates. A policy of 'three 90-per cent' was adopted: • 90 per cent of profit was to be retained by the MPT (in other words, the tax rate is 10 per cent, well below the 55 per cent tax rate for other industries before 1994); • 90 per cent of foreign exchange (hard currency) earnings were to be retained by the MPT; and • 90 per cent of central government investment was not considered as repayable loans.

1983–85   The MPT introduced a revenue-based independent accounting system to PTEs.

1988   The State Council announced the '16-character policy' for telecom infrastructure development, which outlined four principles:

                 • Overall planning of industrial development should be unified under the MPT.
                 • Ministerial administration should be coordinated with regional authorities.
                 • Responsibilities should be defined and shared among different administrative levels.
                 • Construction of infrastructure should mobilize resources from all concerned.

                 The MPT:

                 • granted its national manufacturing, construction and purchasing departments the status of separate legal entities or greater independence in accounting and human resource management;
                 • set up the Directorate General of Telecommunications (DGT) and the Directorate General of Posts (DGP) to incorporate business enterprise functions.

1989   The MPT instructed all province-level post and telecom administrations (PTAs) to set up telecom regulatory bodies.

                 The MPT introduced a terminal equipment licensing scheme that deregulated the use of terminal equipment.

December 1990   The intra-city telephone rates were widely adjusted. Local telecom companies were authorized to:

                 • set their own intra-city rates not exceeding the cap set by the MPT;
                 • charge cost-based installation fees.

1991   The State Council introduced coordinating tax for directions of fixed capital investment. Post and telecom projects were granted the most favourable zero-rate status.

1990–93   Non-MPT suppliers of value-added services, mobile telephone service and satellite communications service emerged and became prevalent in some regions.

June 1992   The MPT stipulated the 'Re-statement on Forbidding Joint Operation of Postal and Telecommunications Business with Foreign Companies'.

May 1993   The MPT restated: 'no organization, enterprise or individual outside China may engage in the management of China's broadcasting networks, special wire or wireless services, or become a shareholder in a telecommunications business'.

July 1993   All PTEs established the capital account system to manage infrastructure development funds.

               The MPT accelerated (accounting) depreciation of telecom capital (equipment: 5–7 years, network 10–15 years).

September 1993 The State Council issued a Directive on Strengthening Regulations in the Management of Telecommunications Sector, formally deregulated the paging market and the VSAT communications by authorizing MPT to license these service suppliers.

April 1994   The MPT awarded a basic telecom licence to China Unicom and a value-added network operating licence to Jitong Communications Company Limited (Beijing).

               Nationwide tax reform unified the corporate tax rates into an across-the-board 33 per cent rate for all enterprises. RMB became convertible for current account transactions.

1994   The MPT froze all subsidiaries' employment and revised PTEs' wage fund–revenue linkage formula to give larger weight to local revenue.

               The government announced the 'eight policies of

telecommunications development' (ref. p. 38).

September 1994   The MPT specified two measures to reward non-MPT investors in trial projects of joint venture: fixed-rate remuneration and dividend distribution.

1995   The MPT's DGT formally registered with the government as China Telecom for the first time as an enterprise legal person.

                 Local postal and telecom enterprises started the process of 'corporatization' under China's Corporation Law.

                 The MPT revised the PTEs' wage fund–performance linkage formula to restrain the employment of new staff and to encourage cost control.

June 1995   The State Council promulgated the *Catalogue of Industries for Guiding Foreign-funded Investment*, which banned foreign direct investment in the telecom service sector.

October 1997   China Telecom launched 144 million initial public offering (IPO) shares in the Hong Kong stock market. The company was formed from several provincial global system for mobile communications (GSM) networks, with China Telecom holding 51 per cent of shares and other shares floating on the Hong Kong stock market.

1995–1998   China Unicom involved 45 Chinese-Chinese-Foreign (CCF) joint ventures to develop and operate wireless and fixed-line networks. In total, 40 companies invested US$ 1.4 billion.

Early 1998   China Telecom introduced the Personal Handyphone System ('*Xiao Ling Tong*') in some small cities.

March 1998   The 9th National People's Congress formed the Ministry of Information Industry (MII) by merging the MPT with the Ministry of Electronics Industry (MEI) and the Network Department of Ministry of Radio, Film and Television (MRFT). Former MPT head Wu Jichuan was installed as MII Minister.

May 1998   The State Administration of Radio, Film and Television (SARFT) announced a plan to proceed with the construction of its national CATV network. The announcement was publicly and forcefully opposed by the MII on the grounds that the plan blatantly violated the MII's authority over the nationwide network development.

July 1998   China Unicom was allowed to interconnect with China Telecom's network in Tianjin.

October 1998   The MII declared the CCF ventures to be illegal and in violation of China's ban on foreign investment in the telecom service sector.

December 1998   The MII issued a new regulation entitled the 'Arrangements for the Approval of Network Access of Telecommunications Equipment' to be effective from 1 January 1999. Under the approval regulation, all telecom equipment to be used in public or private telecom networks in China must obtain a Network Access Licence (NAL) and a Network Access Identifier (NAI) from the MII.

January 1999   The State Council considered a plan to divest China Telecom into four separate commercial entities by sector – namely, fixed-line communications, mobile communications, paging and satellite transmission.

February 1999   Premier Zhu Rongji approved China Network Communication Corporation (China Netcom) in principle as the country's third major telecom company.

     The MII won the State Council's approval for its 'vertical divestiture' plan for splitting China Telecom into four companies.

     The MII decreed that China Unicom must unwind all of its CCF contracts.

March 1999   The State Council slashed Internet connection fees by half, lowered fixed-line and long-distance telephone charges, and reduced mobile phone usage fees and activation fees. The State Council authorized China Unicom to gain a larger share of the mobile phone market and to become the sole operator of code division multiple access (CDMA) that would compete with China Telecom's GSM network. The MII transferred the entire assets of China Telecom's CDMA Great Wall Network and Guoxin Paging Company paging branch to Unicom.

April 1999   China Netcom Corporation was awarded a telecom licence in leasing network lines and offering an Internet protocol (IP) telephone service. Its pledged start-up capital of RMB 420 million came from the Chinese Academy of Sciences, the SARFT, the Ministry of Railways and the Shanghai Municipal Government. Each held a 20 per cent ownership stake in the new company.

Premier Zhu Rongji, during a visit to the US, offered for the first time up to 49 per cent foreign ownership for basic telecom services and 51 per cent foreign ownership for value-added and paging services within four years as part of the concessions to win US approval for China's WTO entry.

May 1999   China Unicom revealed a plan to invest RMB 7 billion (US$ 843 million) to build a CDMA mobile phone network.

The State Development and Planning Commission (SDPC) ratified China Netcom's start-up project, the Broadband Internet Protocol Network Model Project. The RMB 300 million (US$ 36 million) project will build a backbone network, linking 15 major cities in the eastern part of China, including Beijing, Shanghai and Guangzhou.

China Netcom hired Edward Tian, formerly president of the Asiainfo Computer Network Company Limited in Beijing as chief executive officer, marking for the first time a private entrepreneur running a state telecom company.

China's Ministry of Railways announced a plan to upgrade its existing fixed-line network and was poised to become a new carrier in China's telecom business.

The SARFT planned to move into the telecom business by setting up the 'China Cable Television Networks Corporation' and taking advantage of its national cable business networks.

China Telecom and Jitong Communications started the sale of the IP phone card. China Unicom announced the introduction of its IP card in early June. The three IP companies' phone service was to cover over 20 cities.

The State Council approved China Unicom to become the country's fifth Internet operator, the other four being SCTNET, CHINANET, CHINAGBN and CERNET.

AT&T of the US was allowed to build and operate an IP network in Pudong, Shanghai – the first time a foreign operator had been allowed to offer telecom services in its own right.

Hongkong Telecom changed its name to Cable & Wireless HKT.

Several Internet content service joint ventures involving foreign companies were launched.

July 1999   The MII approved China Unicom's plan to build long-distance networks in 25 cities in China.

Internet subscribers in China reached four million.

China Telecom's fixed-line network subscribers exceeded 100 million.

China Unicom terminated CCF contracts with its joint venture partners but won state approval to seek listing in Hong Kong and overseas markets.

China Unicom's IP telephone trial networks were operational in 12 cities.

August 1999   The MII ordered all CCF contracts to be terminated by the end of September.

October 1999 China Unicom stopped distributing payments to CCF foreign joint venture partners.

China Telecom (HK) Limited announced a plan to acquire three Chinese mobile phone networks (in Fujian, Hainan and Henan provinces) from its mainland parent for HK$ 49.72 billion (US$ 6.4 billion) in cash and shares.

November 1999 China signed the World Trade Organization (WTO) accord with the US, in which China committed itself to allow up to 49 per cent of foreign ownership and control in basic telecom service ventures and 50 per cent in value-added services after its accession to the WTO according to an agreed timetable.

The MII announced cuts to telecom charges, including Internet dial-up charges, rents for telephone lines, fixed-line installation charges and charges for a packet-switching service.

Imminent WTO entry sparked a price war between China Telecom and China Unicom. MII planned to set prices for telecom services after intervening to halt the price war.

December 1999 The State Council formed the National Informatization Leading Group, chaired by Vice-Premier Wu Bangguo and vice-chaired by Wu Jichuan, the Minister of MII.

China Netcom became the fourth Chinese company to sell Internet telephone cards, after China Telecom, Unicom and Jitong.

China Unicom unveiled plans to capture more than 30 per cent of the mainland's mobile phone and Internet-related services markets over the next five years, focusing on the expansion of mobile phone and data communications services while selectively developing long-distance and local fixed-line operations.

January 2000 China Unicom signed an interconnection agreement with China Telecom, which enabled it to offer international and domestic long-distance phone services, pending approval from the MII.

China Internet subscribers reached 8.9 million.
The State Secrets Bureau issued the 'State Secrecy
Protection Regulations for Computer Information Systems
on the Internet'.

February 2000   China Telecom (HK) overtook HSBC to become the largest
company in Hong Kong's stock market, having a market
capitalization of HK$ 822.37 billion.

March 2000   The MII allowed China Unicom to provide international
direct dial (IDD) service.

China Unicom obtained a record loan of US$ 1.2 billion
(RMB 10 billion) from the China Development Bank. The
Bank of China gave China Unicom a RMB 1.6 billion
credit line as part of a RMB 22 billion lending package.

China Unicom agreed compensation with more than 30
foreign companies over CCF joint ventures banned by the
MII.

April 2000   The MII issued four IP telephony licences to China
Telecom, China Unicom, Jitong Corporation and China
Netcom.

China Telecom was divested into two phone companies,
China Telecommunications (Group) Company [with a
registered capital of RMB 220 billion (US$ 26.5 billion)]
and China Mobile Telecommunications (Group) Company
[with a registered capital of RMB 51.8 billion (US$ 6.2
billion)] – the former took over fixed-line services, while
the latter handled mobile phone business. China Unicom
took over the former monopoly's paging business, while a
satellite carrier was expected to be launched soon.

China Unicom applied for a dual listing in the US and Hong
Kong, seeking to raise US$ 4–5 billion from the IPO.

Jitong Communications, with total assets of RMB 1 billion
(US$ 121 million), disclosed plans to list on Hong Kong's

Growth Enterprise Market and on NASDAQ.

May 2000   The Sino–European Union accord on China's WTO entry
                  was signed. The deal further accelerated the opening in
                  mobile telephony by two years. Foreign ownership of up to
                  25 per cent would be allowed upon accession, 35 per cent
                  after one year and 49 per cent after three years. Leasing and
                  resale of telecom circuits would be allowed for foreign
                  firms in three years after China's accession to the WTO.

                  China's 50 million mobile phone users increased the
                  country's telephone business volume above that of fixed
                  phone services for the first time in the first quarter of the
                  year.

                  China Mobile Communications (Group) Corporation
                  acquired at no cost China Telecom Group's stake in China
                  Telecom (HK) Company Limited and hence became the
                  new owner of China Telecom (HK), which changed its
                  name to China Mobile (HK).

                  The China Telecom Group planned to slash its international
                  call charges by as much as 50 per cent in order to strengthen
                  its hold on the telecom market, as well as to cancel
                  telephone installation fees and restructure charges for city
                  calls from three-minute blocks to single minutes.

                  China Netcom planned to invest US$ 2.5 billion over the
                  next five years to build a nationwide broadband backbone
                  network.

                  China Unicom launched the wireless application protocol
                  (WAP) network in 20 Chinese cities, which would allow its
                  mobile phone users to access information on the Internet.
                  The MII issued an order to halt the service of the PHS
                  ['*Xiao Ling Tong*' (personal handyphone service)]
                  nationwide for further reviews and to ban unapproved
                  construction and operation of the PHS without approval.

June 2000   China Unicom confirmed that it would not use
                  Qualcomm's CDMA technology for its cellular phone
                  market for at least three years. Instead, China Unicom will

use its own proprietary technology known as TD-CDMA.

China Unicom launched a record US$ 5 billion IPO in Hong Kong and New York, the biggest by a Chinese company and the largest ever Asian IPO outside Japan.

China Mobile (HK) prepared to purchase seven of the mainland's biggest provincial and municipal mobile phone networks from its state-owned parent, China Mobile Communications Corporation. The covered regions included Beijing, Tianjin, Shanghai, Liaoning, Hebei, Shandong and Guangxi.

China's mobile phone users topped 60 million at the end of June, outnumbering Japan's 51 million to become the largest mobile phone market in the Asia-Pacific region.

The MII promulgated the 'Notice on Regulating PHS Development and Operation', which sanctioned the PHS as a 'supplement to and extension of fixed-line telephony', with 'small-scope, slow-mobility and wireless connections to the network'.

July 2000   China Mobile and China Unicom signed an agreement to ensure interconnection between their networks. The agreement would help standardize their services and raise the quality of inter-network telephone services.

Cable & Wireless HKT approved its merger plan with the Internet investment group Pacific Century CyberWorks Limited.

August 2000   Jitong Communications Company Limited signed an agreement with ITXC Corporation to send and receive international voice and fax calls to and from China with each other over ITXC.net(TM), the world's largest IP network.

A Hong Kong court approved the acquisition of Cable & Wireless HKT by Pacific Century Cyberworks, which undertook a $38.1 billion bid.

September 2000 State Council approved the *Telecommunications Regulations,* which provides the industry with a principal legal framework.

Lycos Incorporation's affiliate in Asia received a licence from the Chinese authorities to operate one of China's first foreign-owned websites.

The MII renewed the country's commitment to narrowband CDMA, the mobile telephony technology developed by Qualcomm.

China Telecom planned to spin off non-core businesses and shift about 200,000 staff from its payroll as part of a plan to turn itself into an 'internationally competitive' company within five years.

Telephone subscribers in China reached 200 million, of which 135 million were fixed-line users and 65 million mobile phone users.

October 2000   China Unicom announced its plan to deploy the CDMA network, paving the way for Qualcomm to enter China's market.

Foreign firms Lucent Technologies, Motorola and Texas Instruments were allowed to manufacture mobile phones in China.

The MII announced its telecom price-cut package, a proposal submitted by Wu Jichuan to the State Council, in which the fixed-line installation fees of RMB 1,000 and mobile service access fees of RMB 500 would be scrapped. Vodafone invested US$ 2.5 billion for a 2 per cent stake in China Mobile (Hong Kong).

November 2000 China Netcom Corporation started a trial operation of its broadband high-speed network, CNCnet, which covered 17 cities in eastern and southern China and had a total length of approximately 8,000 km (4,968 miles).

MII planned to set up a 'universal service fund' to boost

telecom development in China's western regions including Xinjiang and Tibet.

December 2000   US telecom giant AT&T became the first foreign carrier to start a telecom service joint venture in China, with Shanghai Telecom and Shanghai Information Investment, to provide broadband value-added services to businesses in Shanghai's Pudong area.

China PTIC Information Industry, the country's largest manufacturer of telecom equipment, planned for a listing in Hong Kong.

The MII, SDPC and Ministry of Finance jointly released a plan to slash telecom charges by more than 50 per cent, including international and domestic long-distance calls, calls made between mainland China, Hong Kong, Macau and Taiwan, Internet surfing charges and price of leased-line services. In addition, the surcharges for basic telephony services would be abolished while fixed-line tariff would be charged at a flat rate of RMB 100 per month.

China's mobile phone subscribers almost doubled from the previous year to 85 million.

January 2001   The People's Liberation Army (PLA) officially transferred its mobile network to China Unicom.

China Mobile and Netease.com started an online short message service enabling mobile phone subscribers to send text messages through the Internet.

China Railcom was officially licensed by the MII to provide basic fixed-line (local and long-distance) telecom service, Internet access and IP telephony.

February 2001   A price war in IP business loomed with China Netcom slashing its price of long-distance IP calls by 50 per cent. China Telecom, China Unicom and Jitong Communications followed suit by offering discounts for their IP cards.

China Unicom introduced discounted tariff packages, which included long-distance calls, IDD calls, calls to and from Hong Kong, Macau and Taiwan and IP telephony subscription fees.

China Telecom introduced a pre-paid card that could provide Chinese residents travelling abroad cheaper Internet access via local providers in other countries.

Silk Road Technologies of the US opened an Internet data centre in Hangzhou city to provide website hosting services.

China Telecom planned to complete a broadband fibre-optic network in three to five years.

The MII gave the command that the PHS phone monthly subscription should be set either at RMB 25 with a per-minute rate of RMB 0.20 or at RMB 35 with a per-minute rate of RMB 0.15.

March 2001   China Railcom officially started operations to offer basic telecom services such as domestic long-distance calls, local telephone calls, data transmission and Internet services.

China Mobile offered a seven-tier tariff package for its customers in response to China Unicom's earlier tariff cuts.

China Telecom signed a contract worth US $44 million with Canada's Nortel Networks to install and upgrade fibre-optic networks in Hebei, Jiangsu and Jiangxi provinces.

Jitong Communications concluded an equity deal with Harbin-based private firm Orient Group, China's first domestic private firm to enter the country's telecom sector.

China Telecom slashed IP charges on international calls by up to 50 per cent.

China Telecom signed an agreement with France's Alcatel SA which would supply more than 50 per cent of the equipment to deploy high-speed Internet access.

April 2001   China Mobile and China Unicom announced plans to issue 'A' shares on the domestic stock market for raising funds.

The MII and SDPC jointly issued a notice demanding an immediate halt to unauthorized long-distance fibre-optic cable projects. The notice also reiterated that entities from foreign countries, as well as Hong Kong, Macau and Taiwan, were not allowed to make any direct investment in telecom network construction, operation and management before China joins the WTO.

China's mobile phone users reached 105 million.

May 2001   CITIC Pacific planned to form a joint venture with the Dalian government to connect the city's households to the broadband information highway.

China Mobile planned to provide 2.5 generation (2.5G) of mobile telecom services.

June 2001   China Unicom's HK arm laid off more than 3,000 personnel in the first half of 2001.

China Telecom and China Railcom signed a network interconnection agreement.

China Mobile to pay 4 per cent interest, through its Guangdong Mobile Communication unit, for its first RMB-denominated guaranteed bonds issue, which it planned to use for the acquisition of additional mobile operations in seven provinces.

MII issued notice for trial opening of the residential broadband market in 13 Chinese cities. Eligible non-infrastructure telecom operators other than China Telecom and China Unicom were allowed to enter the market.

China Netcom forged a strategic alliance with Singapore Telecom (SingTel), enabling the former to provide data transmission services linking Singapore-based companies and their subsidiaries and partners in China.

China Unicom registered 30 million mobile phone subscribers, with market share reaching 24 per cent.

MII announced a RMB 120 billion (US$ 14.5 billion) telecom network upgrading plan for China's autonomous regions – Inner Mongolia, Guangxi, Ningxia, Xinjiang and Tibet.

July 2001   The MII and Ministry of Finance jointly abolished the installation fee for fixed telephone lines and network access fee for mobile phones.

The MII lifted restrictions on IP telephone rates for telecom operators.

The MII put forward a 'mutual entry' proposal suggesting that the telecom network and cable television network should be allowed to spread intersectional business under the same condition.

China overtook the US as the world's largest mobile phone market after registering 120.6 million mobile phone subscribers, compared to the US's 120.1 million.

August 2001   China Railcom signed interconnection agreements with several operators in 16 provinces and cities, removing barriers in its bid to become the country's second largest fixed-line operator.

China Telecom postponed its overseas IPO plan until 2002 due to a government dispute over its restructuring.

The MII announced new rules to weed out unlicensed operators from unauthorized telecom network investment and requested all joint ventures to apply for a separate licence for continuing operations.

September 2001 The State Leading Group for Informatization, a supra-ministry panel headed by Premier Zhu Rongji, was set up to oversee the info-communications industry. The

National Informatization Promotion Office, headed by Zeng Peiyan, Minister of the SDPC, was set up as a special office under the State Council to implement policies and measures in the drive for informatization.

China's telephone users passed the 300 million mark, with China Telecom having 171 million fixed-line users at the end of September.

October 2001   The State Council decided to split China Telecom into two regional companies along north–south lines. The second divestiture of China Telecom would lead to the merger of the northern spin-off from the China Telecom with China Netcom, while the new China Telecom will operate the remaining network in southern provinces.

The MII ordered a halt to the price war between China Mobile and China Unicom.

China Mobile signed a contract with Motorola for expanding and upgrading its general packet radio service (GPRS) network.

France's Alcatel took over control of its Shanghai joint venture with a US$ 312 million majority stake following the setting-up of Alcatel Shanghai Bell (ASB).

December 2001   China officially becomes a member of the WTO.

The State Council promulgated the *Regulations on Foreign-invested Telecom Enterprises*, which mirrored China's WTO accession terms by allowing foreign direct investment in telecom service provision but keeping foreign telecom players from owning majority stakes in mobile or basic telecom infrastructure operators.

China Satellite Communications Corporation (China Satcom) was officially set up to provide a general network service, a broadband access service, an IP basic service and an IP value-added service in one or two years.

China Telecom's PHS telephony had been available in

more than 100 cities and localities in 28 provinces, with over four million users.

January 2002   The MII issued the No.19 Ministerial Decree to promulgate the *Regulations on the Licence for Operation of Telecommunications Business.*

The MII and SDPC jointly promulgated the *Provisions of Telecom Network Construction* to take effect in February.

The MII proposed setting up a universal service fund.

China Unicom launched the first nationwide CDMA network in China.

March 2002   AT&T officially launched telecom services in Shanghai through a joint venture, Shanghai Symphony Telecommunications. It holds a 25 per cent share in the company, with Shanghai Telecom holding 60 per cent and Shanghai Information Investment holding 15 per cent.

May 2002   The new China Telecom (with 70 per cent of China Telecom's network asset) and China Netcom Corporation (with 30 per cent of China Telecom's network asset) officially launched under the names of 'China Telecom Corporation' and 'China Netcom Communication Group Corporation', respectively. The second divestiture of China Telecom concluded.

Alcatel Shanghai Bell (in which Alcatel holds 51 per cent share) was officially launched in Shanghai as a 'strong and advanced manufacturing centre'.

June 2002   The number of GSM and CDMA mobile telephone users reached 176 million.

July 2002   The SDPC and MII jointly circulated a catalogue of telecom service fees to be market-coordinated. Telecom operators were allowed to set service rates/prices within the range of businesses specified by the catalogue.

Pacific Century CyberWorks formed a RMB 200 million (US$ 24 million) joint venture with China Telecom to provide IT services to China's financial sector. The Hong Kong company took 48.5 per cent share of the joint venture.

China overtook the US as world's largest telephone market, with total number of telephone users reaching 380 million.

August–   Several projects with foreign participation were
September 2002 announced, including the construction of a 17-city broadband network (jointly invested by China Netcom and Equant) catering for commercial users, expandable to cover 26 other cities by the year end; China Unicom's CDMA network based on binary runtime environment for wireless (BREW), to be developed with Qualcomm by the year end; and Unicom's US$ 40-million contract with Nortel Networks to expand GSM networks in west China.

The SDPC and MII jointly promulgated the *Provisions of Approval and Filing Procedures of Telecom Service Rates* and the *List of Telecommunications Service Rates to be Co-determined by Provincial Communications Administrations and the Provincial Price Regulatory Authorities*.

September 2002 The PHS users in China exceeded the 10-million threshold and the service was available in 400 cities.

October 2002   Due to slack demand, China Telecom pulled off its plan to launch its IPO for 16.8 billion shares in New York and Hong Kong in November 2002, which was supposed to raise US$ 3.68 billion.

November 2002 China Telecom relaunched its IPO with a 55 per cent cut in the number of shares offering to raise US$ 1.65 billion instead. The newly listed overseas branch had China Telecom's network assets in Guangdong, Jiangsu, Zhejiang and Shanghai. The share price suffered a 5.37 per cent drop on the first day of trading despite the last-minute moves by the MII to implement an eightfold increase in foreign carriers' termination rates into China.

China Netcom Corp set up eight provincial branch

companies in southern China.

December 2002   China Telecom and China Netcom Corp signed agreements on 'network resource cooperation' and 'interconnection arrangements between branch companies in several provinces'.

China Telecom set up a subsidiary in the Hebei province, the first in northern China.

January 2003   UTStarcom won a deal worth US$ 71.5 million for China Telecom's PHS network in provinces of Shaanxi and Wuhan. UTStarcom also obtained an order from China Netcom to provide US$114 million worth of PHS equipment for *Xiao Ling Tong* services in provinces of Hebei, Shandong and Liaoning.

Unicom announced it had reached its target of 7 million CDMA users.

SK Telecom, Korea's largest mobile carrier, signed an agreement with China Unicom to establish a wireless Internet joint venture focus on CDMA 1x business in China. SK Telecom would take a 49 per cent stake in the joint venture, while China Unicom would have the remaining 51 per cent.

The Beijing Telecom Administration fined China Unicom RMB 300,000 (US$ 36,245) for tariff violations related to promotional packages offered on the carrier's GSM network. The violation was related to offering much larger discounts than the 10 per cent discount allowed by MII vis-à-vis the prices of its competitor China Mobile.

Guangdong Telecom, a provincial subsidiary of China Telecom, launched a controversial call-forwarding service in three cities in Guangdong whereby mobile users can forward incoming calls to fixed-line phones without paying the called-party fee or the call-forwarding fee, which the mobile operators charge. The news caused shares of Unicom and China Mobile to tumble.

February 2003   Qualcomm Incorporated and China Unicom announced a joint venture – Unicom-BREW Wireless Technologies Ltd. – to foster the development of CDMA wireless data applications based on a binary runtime environment for the wireless (BREW) platform.

MII set rules for upgrading seven-digit telephone numbers to eight-digit numbers for local exchanges.

China Telecom and China Netcom Corp implemented the interconnection arrangement between their branches in Shanghai.

March 2003   Wu Jichuan, the outgoing Minister of Information Industry, said that the MII policy towards PHS (*Xiao Ling Tong*) service was 'neither encouraging nor intervening'.

Wang Xudong, an official with no post telecom administration background, was elected Minister of Information Industry at the First Plenary of the 10th National People's Congress.

MII promulgated the Telecom Service Classification List, which reclassifies 'basic telecom services' and 'value-added services'. PHS (*Xiao Ling Tong*) service is noticeably missing from the list but a more liberal definition of the fixed-line service may be interpreted for allowing the PHS service. The new list also sanctions the 3G telephony.

MII ordered fixed-line operators (China Telecom and CNC) to dismantle some of their wireless local loop operations (*Xiao Ling Tong*) based in the 450 MHz band using CDMA technology within one month.

MII started a research project to re-evaluate the interconnection charge accounting system.

UTStarcom won a US$40 million contract with China Telecom for new and expansion deployments of its PHS equipment in the Jiangsu and Guangdong provinces.

April 2003   China Unicom announced it had completed upgrading its nationwide CDMA network to CDMA 1x, enabling a host of new mobile services, including multimedia messages and high-speed Internet access.

MII's existing deputy minister Zhang Chunjiang was reappointed as China Netcom Corp's new chief executive officer while Xi Guohua, Netcom's exiting chief executive officer, was reappointed as MII's new deputy minister.

May 2003   China Telecom set up branches in three northern provinces of Liaoning, Tianjin and Shandong.

PHS (*Xiao Ling Tong*) users reached 16 million while the service started to be available in mega cities, including Chongqing, Guangzhou, Beijing and Shanghai.

In response to fixed-line operators' *Xiao Ling Tong* and mobile-to-fixed telephone call-forwarding services, China Unicom and China Mobile had announced service packages in the past weeks that de facto scrapped receiver-party fees for mobile telephone users in Guandong, Shanghai and Beijing. These 'quasi-one-way fee' packages had broken the long-held MII policy of the two-way fee structure for mobile telephony.

China Unicom's CDMA network customer base had surpassed 10 million.

China Telecom and China Netcom Corp implemented interconnection agreements in all their local branches.

June 2003   China Telecom had set up provincial branches in all the ten northern provinces in the fixed-line network territory of China Netcom Corp.

By the end of June 2003, China's fixed-line telephone subscribers reached 238 million, mobile telephone users reached 234 million, and Internet subscribers reached 68 million (of which 3.2 million were broadband users). Penetration rate reached 19.4 per cent for fixed-line telephone service and 18.3 per cent for mobile telephone service. 87.9 per cent of administrative villages in rural area had telephone connections.

Source: *Yearbook of China Transportation and Communications,* various years; *China Online News,* http://www.chinaonline.com; *China Telecom Weekly News* (Boston); *South China Morning Post* (Hong Kong); *China Telecom E-News* (Boston); *The MII Web Site News,* http://www.mii.gov.cn; *China Communications News,* www.c114.net; Global Wireless.com.

Appendix 2. Telecommunications regulations of the People's Republic of China

(Passed at the 31st Standing Session of the State Council on 20 September 2000 and promulgated on 25 September 2000)

CHAPTER ONE   GENERAL PRINCIPLES

Article 1. This set of regulations is formulated to standardize the order of the telecommunications (telecom hereafter) market, safeguard the legitimate interests of both subscribers and operators of telecom services, and ensure the security of telecom networks and information so as to promote the healthy development of telecom activities in the country.

Article 2. This set of regulations must be abided by in conducting telecom business or telecom related activities within the People's Republic of China.

Telecommunications mentioned in this set of regulations refer to acts of remitting, transmitting or receiving voice, text, data, images, or information in any other forms via the wire or wireless electromagnetic system or the photoelectric system.

Article 3. The department in charge of the information industry under the State Council is entitled to exercise supervision and regulation over the country's telecom industry in accordance with this set of regulations.

Offices in charge of telecom regulation at the level of provinces, autonomous regions and municipalities (hereinafter referred to as telecom regulatory offices at the provincial level) are required to exercise supervision and regulation over the telecom industry within their respective administrative regions under the leadership of the department in charge of the information industry of the State Council in accordance with this set of regulations.

Article 4. The principles of separating governmental functions from business operations, eliminating monopoly, encouraging competition, promoting development and being open, fair and just should be followed in exercising supervision and regulation over the telecom industry.

Telecom business operators should operate their business in accordance with laws and business ethics, subject to legitimate supervisions and inspections.

Article 5. Telecom business operators should offer rapid, accurate, secured, convenient, and reasonably priced telecom services to their subscribers.

Article 6. Security of telecom network and information is protected by law. No organization or individual should use the telecom network to engage in activities that would harm the national security, social public welfare or legitimate rights of others.

CHAPTER TWO: TELECOM MARKET

Section One   Telecom Licences

Article 7. The state implements the licensing scheme over telecom business operations in accordance with a classification of telecom business.

A telecom business operator must obtain a telecom licence from the department in charge of the information industry under the State Council or from departments in charge of the information industry at the provincial level in accordance with this set of regulations.

No organization or individual should conduct telecom business without a telecom licence.

Article 8. Telecom business is classified into basic telecom business and value-added telecom business.

Basic telecom business refers to those which provide infrastructure to public telecom networks, transmission of public data and basic voice communications services. Value-added business refers to those which provide telecom and information services via the infrastructure of public telecom networks.

The detailed classification of telecom business will be specified in the 'Catalogue of Classification of Telecom Business' as an annex to this set of regulations. The department in charge of the information industry under the State Council may according to specific conditions partly adjust the categories of telecom business listed in the Catalogue and re-announce the results.

Article 9. Operators of basic telecom business must, upon examination of and approval from the department in charge of the information industry under the State Council, acquire a 'licence for basic telecom business'.

Operators of value-added telecom business in more than two provinces, autonomous regions and municipalities must, upon examination of and approval from the department in charge of the information industry under the State Council, acquire a 'licence for cross-regional value-added telecom business'.

Operators that try new types of telecom business not listed in the 'Catalogue of Classification of Telecom Business' with new technologies must report to the telecom regulatory offices at provincial, autonomous region or municipality level for documentation and filing.

Article 10. The following terms and conditions should be met for operating basic telecom business:

1. The operator concerned must be a legally established company dealing specifically in basic telecom business, and that its state-owned stocks or shares must not be less than 51 per cent;
2. There is a feasibility study report and a technical programme for network building;
3. There are sufficient funds and professionals required for business operations;
4. There are suitable sites and corresponding resources for business operations;
5. The operator has the reputation or capability to provide long-term services to subscribers;
6. Other terms and conditions stipulated by the State.

Article 11. When applying to operate basic telecom business, an application form together with related documents mentioned in Article 10 of this set of regulations should be filed to the department in charge of the information industry under the State Council. The department in charge of the information industry under the State Council shall complete its examination of the application within 180 days of receiving the application and make a decision on whether or not to approve the application. One that is approved will be granted a 'licence for basic telecom business'; and one that is not should be notified with a written explanation.

Article 12. In examining an application for operating basic telecom business, the department in charge of the information industry under the State Council should take into consideration factors such as national security, telecom network security, the sustainable use of telecom resources, environmental protection and competition in the telecom market.

Article 13. The following terms and conditions should be met in operating value-added telecom business:

1. The operator must be a legally established company;
2. There are sufficient funds and professionals required for business operations;
3. The operator has the reputation or capability to provide long-term services to subscribers;
4. Other terms and conditions stipulated by the State.

Article 14. When applying to operate value-added telecom business, an application form together with the related documents specified in Article 13 of this set of Regulations must be filed to the department in charge of the information industry under the State Council or at provincial, autonomous region and municipality level according to the stipulations of Clause 2 of Article 9 of this set of regulations. The operator concerned, which has to be examined and approved by related administrative organs according to the State stipulations, should also submit approval documents issued by the relevant administrative departments. The department in charge of information industry under the State Council or the telecom regulatory offices at provincial, autonomous region and municipality level should complete its work of examining the application within 60 days of receiving the application and make a decision on whether or not to approve the application. One that is approved will be granted a 'licence for cross-regional value-added telecom business' or a 'licence for value-added telecom business' and one that is not approved should be notified with a written explanation.

Article 15. The telecom business operator that changes its main operations or business scope, or terminates business in the process of operation should file an application to the original licence-granting authorities 90 days in advance and handle the corresponding procedure. In the case of a termination of operations, the follow-up work should be handled in accordance with the State's related stipulations.

Article 16. An operator approved to provide telecom services should hold the licence for telecom business operations acquired in accordance with laws and handle the registration procedure with the corporation registration authority.

To operate a specialized network in its own locality, an application should be filed in accordance with the terms and conditions and procedures specified in this set of regulations upon approval to obtain a licence for telecom business. The registration procedure will then be handled in accordance with the stipulations of the previous article.

Section Two   Interconnection of Telecom Networks

Article 17. Telecom networks should be interconnected based on the principles of 'technical feasibility, economic rationality, fairness and justice, and mutual cooperation'.

A dominant telecom business operator must not refuse the request for interconnection put forth by other telecom businesses and specialized telecom network operators.

The dominant telecom business operator mentioned in the previous clause refers to an operator that can influence entry into the telecom market by other telecom business operators through its dominance of the essential telecom infrastructure and occupies a relatively large share of the telecom market.

Dominant telecom operators shall be determined by the department in charge of the information industry under the State Council.

Article 18. A dominant telecom business operator should draft the interconnection programme, including network interconnection procedures, time limit, catalogue of unbundling network elements based on the principles of non-discrimination and transparency. The interconnection programme should be reported to the department in charge of the information industry under the State Council for examination and approval. Such interconnection programme shall constrain the interconnection operations of the dominant telecom business operators.

Article 19. The parties involved in network interconnection between public telecom networks or between a public and a specialized telecom network shall negotiate for an interconnection agreement in accordance with the network interconnection regulations issued by the department in charge of the information industry under the State Council.

The network interconnection agreement should be filed with the department in charge of the information industry under the State Council.

Article 20. Where the two parties involved in network interconnection are unable to reach an agreement through negotiations within 60 days from the day when one of the parties proposed the interconnection, any of the parties may apply for mediation from the department in charge of information industry under the State Council or the telecom regulatory offices at provincial level, in accordance with the scope covered by the interconnected networks. The authority receiving the application should conduct mediation based on the principles specified in Clause 1 of Article 17 of this set of regulations to conclude an agreement for network interconnection between the parties. Where an agreement still cannot be concluded within 45 days from the day when one or both of the two parties applied for mediation, the mediating authority should at its discretion invite experts on telecom technologies and on other aspects to propose solutions for the network interconnection through open discussion. The mediating authority should enforce the implementation of an interconnection according to the solutions proposed.

Article 21. Parties involved in a network interconnection should implement the interconnection within the period specified by the agreement or the decision. Neither party is allowed to arbitrarily disconnect the networks without approval from the department in charge of information industry under the State Council. Technical barriers to communications should be promptly eliminated by the two parties. Disputes occurring in the course of interconnection should be settled in accordance with the procedures and methods specified in Article 20 of this set of regulations.

The communications quality of the interconnected networks should conform to related standards as set by the State. The quality of services provided by the dominant telecom operator to other telecom operators for network interconnection should not be inferior to those on the network of the dominant operator or those provided by the dominant operator to its affiliates or branches.

Article 22. The settlement and sharing of network interconnection charges should conform to the State's related rules and no surcharge is to be collected beyond the specified standard.

The department in charge of information under the State Council shall be responsible for formulating the technical standards, method of connection charge settlement and the detailed regulatory rules of network interconnection.

Section Three   Telecom Tariffs

Article 23. Telecom tariff standards should be set on the basis of actual costs, and at the same time take into account factors such as the needs of national economic and social development, development of the telecom industry and the affordability of telecom service subscribers.

Article 24. Telecom tariffs are classified as market-coordinated prices, government-guided prices and government-set prices.

Government-set, government-guided or market-coordinated prices shall be adopted for the provision of basic telecom services while market-coordinated prices and government-guided prices shall be adopted for the provision of value-added telecom services.

Where the market has been sufficiently competitive for telecom business, market-coordinated prices shall be adopted.

The catalogues of telecom services subject to market-coordinated prices, government-guided prices and government-set prices shall be formulated and promulgated for implementation by the department in charge of the information industry under the State Council after consulting the pricing department under the State Council.

Article 25. The standards of government-set prices for essential telecom services shall be proposed after consulting the pricing department under the State Council and then promulgated for implementation by the department in charge of information industry under the State Council upon approval by the State Council.

The standard ranges of government-guided prices for telecom services shall be formulated and promulgated for implementation by the department in charge of information industry under the State Council. Within these ranges, the telecom operators may independently determine pricing standards and report the standards to the telecom regulatory offices at provincial level for documentation.

Article 26. The standards of government-set and government-guided prices for telecom services should be formulated after consulting telecom operators, telecom service users and related sectors through procedures such as hearings.

Telecom operators should provide accurate and complete statistical data on cost and other information according to the requirements of the department in charge of the information industry under the State Council or the telecom regulatory offices at provincial level.

Section Four   Telecom Resources

Article 27. The State shall implement a pay-for-use scheme for utilization of telecom resources based on unified planning, centralized management and rational allocation.

Telecom resources mentioned in the previous clause refer to the limited resources of radio frequencies, orbit locations of satellites and telecom network codes that are used for telecom operations.

Article 28. Telecom business operators should pay telecom resource charges for the possession and/or use of telecom resources. Detailed charging methods will be formulated by the department in charge of the information industry under the State Council, together with the finance and pricing departments under the State Council, and will be implemented upon approval by the State Council.

Article 29. Allocation of telecom resources should take into consideration factors such as telecom resource planning, utilization and anticipated service capacity.

Allocation of telecom resources can be accomplished through assignment or public auction.

After obtaining the right to utilize telecom resources, the party concerned should start using the assigned resources within a specified period of time and attain the minimum specified scale of use. Arbitrary use, transfer, lease and/or change of use of telecom resources without approval from the department in charge of the information industry under the State Council or the telecom regulatory offices at the provincial level are not allowed.

Article 30. After a telecom resource user has legally obtained the resources of telecom network codes, the dominant telecom business operator and other related units should take necessary technical measures to coordinate with the telecom resource user's efforts of realizing the functions of its telecom network resources.

Where laws and administrative regulations have other stipulations on the regulation of telecom resources, the stipulations should be followed.

CHAPTER THREE: TELECOM SERVICES

Article 31. A telecom business operator should provide services to its users according to the telecom service standards specified by the State. The telecom business operator should publicize the types, scopes, tariff standards and time schedule of services provided, and report them to the telecom regulatory offices at the provincial level for documentation.

Telecom users have the right to independently select various kinds of telecom services operated legally.

Article 32. Where a telecom user applies for installation or changing the location of telecom terminal equipment, the telecom operator concerned should ensure the installation and turning on of the equipment within the time limit it publicly promised. Where the installation and turning on of equipment cannot be achieved within the time limit due to failures of the telecom operator, the operator should compensate the user with 1 per cent of the installation expenses, location-changing expenses or other expenses on a daily basis.

Article 33. Where a telecom user informs the telecom operator of failures of the telecom services it uses, the telecom operator should resume or turn on the services for successful communication within 48 hours for urban areas and 72 hours for rural areas. Where the operator is not able to resume the services or fails to turn on the communication within the specified period of time, it should notify the user without undue delay and exempt the user from paying monthly rental charges for the period when the service is interrupted unless the troubles are caused by failure associated with the user's terminal equipment.

Article 34. A telecom operator should provide convenience to the telecom user in their payments of fees and enquiries. Where the telecom user requests a list of fees for domestic long-distance phone calls, international phone calls, mobile communications and information services, the list should be provided by the operator free of charge.

Whenever an abnormally large amount of telecom fee charged to a telecom user is discovered, the telecom operator should notify the telecom user and take necessary steps as soon as possible.

The large amount of telecom fee mentioned in the previous clause refers to an abrupt emergence of a fee exceeding five times the average telecom fee of the user during the previous three months.

Article 35. A telecom user should pay telecom fees to the operator concerned on time and in full amount according to the specified time and mode. Whenever the user fails to pay the fees within the specified period of time, the telecom operator is entitled to request the user to pay the fees plus a penalty of 3 per cent of the payable fees everyday.

For a telecom user that fails to pay the due fees 30 days beyond the specified payment period, the telecom operator may suspend the corresponding services. For a telecom subscriber that fails to pay the due fees and penalty 60 days after the suspension of telecom services, the telecom operator may terminate the provision of services and request the payment of fees and the penalties owed in accordance with the laws.

Operators of mobile phone business may specify the terms and mode of payments of telecom fees with the users, and are not subject to the restrictions of the time limit specified in the previous clause.

The telecom business operator should resume the provision of telecom services within 48 hours after the payment of the fees and penalties owed by the corresponding telecom subscriber.

Article 36. A telecom business operator should inform its users and report to the telecom regulatory offices at the provincial level within a specified period of time whenever the provision of normal telecom services is or may be affected for reasons such as project works-in-progress and network construction.

Where the provision of telecom services is interrupted due to reasons mentioned above, the telecom business operator should reduce or exempt the related fees for the service-interruption period accordingly

If the situation mentioned in Clause 1 of this article occurs, the telecom business operator that does not notify its users on time should compensate the latter for the amount of losses they incurred.

Article 37. A telecom business operator that operates the local telephone business and mobile phone business should provide public welfare telecom services such as hotlines for fire alarm, police report, medical emergency and traffic accident alert free of charge and ensure the smooth transmission of the communication lines.

Article 38. A telecom business operator should provide equal, reasonable and timely service to group users for ready access to its telecom network through trunk lines.

No telecom operator is allowed to interrupt the access service without permission.

Article 39. A telecom business operator should establish a complete internal quality control system for its services, and may formulate and implement its own service standards that are higher than those set by the State.

The telecom operator should by all methods listen to suggestions from its users, put itself under social supervision and constantly improve the quality of its telecom services provided.

Article 40. When telecom services provided by a telecom operator fail to meet the standards as announced by the State or by the operator itself or there are objections of the charged payment for telecom service, subscribers have the right to request the telecom operator for a solution. When the telecom operator refuses to solve the problem or the subscribers are not satisfied with the solution offered, the subscriber concerned is entitled to appeal to the department in charge of the information industry under the State Council, or telecom regulatory offices at the provincial level or other related departments. Departments receiving the appeal should handle it timely and reply to the appealing party within 30 days, starting from the day of receiving the appeal.

Where there are objections arising from telecom users in fee payments for local phone calls, the telecom business operator should accede to users' request by giving free advice on the basis for charging local phone call fees and take the necessary steps to find out the reasons for such objections.

Article 41. The following actions are not to be undertaken by telecom business operators:

1. Restricting telecom users' use of assigned services by the subscribers by various means;
2. Restricting the users to purchase telecom terminal equipment appointed by the operators or refusing users' request to use their own telecom terminal equipment that has been permitted access to the telecom network;
3. Violating the State regulations by changing the tariff standard or increasing the tariff rates in disguised forms without authorization;
4. Refusing, delaying or terminating telecom services provided to users without valid reasons;
5. Failing to honour promises made publicly to the telecom users or making false advertisement to mislead users;
6. Creating difficulties for telecom users by unfair means or taking reprisals against users who lodge complaints.

Article 42. The following acts are not to be undertaken by any telecom business operator in the course of operations:

1. Restricting by any means users' choices of services legally provided by other telecom operators;
2. Engaging in unjust cross-subsidization among services provided by itself;
3. Engaging in unfair competition by offering telecom businesses or services at prices below costs in order to squeeze competitors out of business.

Article 43. The department in charge of the information industry under the State Council or telecom regulatory offices at the provincial level shall, according to their responsibility, monitor and inspect the operations of telecom business operators and the quality of telecom services provided by the latter, with the results of the inspections announced publicly.

Article 44. Telecom business operators should fulfil their obligations of providing universal service in accordance with the State regulations.

Departments in charge of information industry under the State Council may specify the universal service requirements assumed by telecom operators through assignment or tendering.

Procedures governing compensation to costs spent for providing universal service shall be drafted by the department in charge of information industry under the State Council, together with the treasury department and price-setting department under the State Council, and promulgated for implementation after being approved by the State Council.

CHAPTER FOUR: TELECOM CONSTRUCTION

Section One   Construction of Telecom Facilities

Article 45. The construction of public telecom networks, specialized telecom networks and transmission networks for radio and television broadcasting should be put under unified planning and industrial regulation by the department in charge of the information industry under the State Council.

For public telecom networks, specialized telecom networks and transmission networks for radio and television broadcasting, which belong to nationwide information network projects or construction projects exceeding the state-defined quota, approvals should be sought from departments in charge of information industry under the State Council before going through the State examination and approval procedure for the basic construction projects.

Basic telecom construction projects should be incorporated into the overall urban planning of local governments at all levels as well as the overall rural and township construction plans.

Article 46. Affiliated telecom facilities should be included in urban, rural and township construction projects. Telecom cables as well as wiring facilities within buildings and telecom pipes within the boundary of construction project sites should be specified in the design document of the construction projects for checking and acceptance together with the projects concerned. The funds needed for their construction should be included in the overall estimated budgets of the projects.

In planning or building roads, bridges, tunnels or subway, the related units or departments should notify the telecom regulatory offices at the provincial level and the telecom operators in advance for reserving space for installing telecom pipes and cable.

Article 47. Operators of basic telecom businesses may install public telecom facilities such as telecom lines or miniature antennas and mobile communications bases on civilian buildings. However, advanced notifications should be given to owners or users of the buildings and usage charges paid to them in accordance with the standards specified by the People's governments of provinces, autonomous regions or municipalities.

Article 48. Signposts should be set up in the construction of hidden telecom facilities underground and underwater as well as aerial telecom facilities in accordance with the State's related regulations. For building seabed telecom cables, operators of basic telecom businesses should obtain approval from the department in charge of the information industry under the State Council, solicit suggestions from the related department and handle formalities involved in accordance to laws. Seabed telecom cables should be specified on the nautical chart by the related department under the State Council.

Article 49. Any unit or individual is not allowed to change or shift the telecom lines and other telecom facilities without authorization. Whenever there is an emergency or necessity to change or shift the facilities, consent should be sought from the owners of telecom facilities. The unit or individual, which proposes to change or shift the facilities, should bear the costs incurred in changing or shifting, and compensate for the resulting economic losses as well.

Article 50. Activities such as construction, production and tree planting should not compromise the security of telecom lines or other telecom facilities or hinder the smooth operation of lines. Whenever the telecom security might be affected, the related telecom operators should be informed in advance and the units or individuals engaged in the activities mentioned above should be responsible for taking the necessary security protection measures.

Parties violating the previous clause by damaging the telecom lines or other telecom facilities or hindering the smooth operation of the lines should be responsible for reinstatement or repair and compensate for resulting economic losses as well.

Article 51. A necessary safety distance between the existing telecom lines and the new ones under construction should be maintained. Where it is difficult to avoid or necessary to cross the existing lines, or where there is a need to use the existing telecom cables, the related parties should conduct negotiations with the owners of the existing telecom lines and sign corresponding agreements. Where an agreement cannot be reached through consultation, the department in charge of the information industry under the State Council or telecom regulatory offices at the provincial level has to mediate and find a solution for the matter according to specific situations.

Article 52. No organization or individual is allowed to prevent or hinder operators of basic telecom businesses from the construction of telecom facilities and providing public telecom services to users in accordance with the laws, unless such activities involve those areas prohibited or restricted by the State.

Article 53. Telecom vehicles used for specialized communications, emergency communications, urgent repair and imminent works may be exempted from the restrictions against the passage of motor vehicles under approval given by public security and transportation regulatory institutions on the precondition that a smooth and safe traffic flow can be maintained.

Section Two   Network Access of Telecom Equipment

Article 54. The State implements a licensing scheme for access to networks by telecom terminal equipment, wireless communication equipment and equipment for network interconnection.

Telecom terminal equipment, wireless communication equipment and equipment for network interconnection should conform to standards specified by the State and be issued the licence for access to networks.

The catalogue for telecom equipment included in the licensing scheme for access to networks shall be formulated and published for implementation by the department in charge of information industry under the State Council, together with the department in charge of product quality under the State Council.

Article 55. Applications for a licence of network access for telecom equipment should be filed to the department in charge of information industry under the State Council, together with an inspection report issued by a telecom equipment testing institution recognized by the department in charge of product quality control under the State Council or a product quality attestation certificate issued by a certification department.

A department in charge of the information industry under the State Council should complete its examination of the application, testing report of the telecom equipment or the product quality attestation certificate within 60 days of receiving the application. By then, a qualified one will be granted a licence of network access while one which fails to pass the inspection should be given a written reply and explanation.

Article 56. Producers of telecom equipment should ensure corresponding reliability and stability of the quality and performance of the licensed telecom equipment for network access and they are not to lower the quality or performance of their products.

Producers of telecom equipment should affix symbols of network access permit onto the telecom equipment they produce.

Departments in charge of product quality inspection under the State Council should conduct follow-up monitoring and inspection on samples of the telecom equipment of network access, together with the department in charge of information industry under the State Council. The results of sampling examination should be announced publicly.

CHAPTER FIVE: TELECOM SECURITY

Article 57. No organization or individual is allowed to use telecom networks to make, copy, release, and disseminate information that contains the following contents:

1.   Running counter to the basic principles specified by the Constitution;
2.   Harming the national security, leaking state secrets, subverting the state's political power, and impeding the country's reunification;
3.   Harming the state reputation and interests;
4.   Instigating ethnic enmity, giving rise to racial discrimination, and harming national solidarity;
5.   Undermining the country's religious policies and disseminating ideas of evil cults and superstitions;
6.   Spreading rumours to disturb the social order and stability;
7.   Spreading pornography, eroticism, gambling, violence, murder, terror or criminality;
8.   Insulting or defaming others and harming the legal interests of others;
9.   Having contents prohibited by the laws and administrative regulations.

Article 58. No organization or individual is allowed to harm the security of telecom network and information by:

1.   Eliminating or altering functions of, data in storage, processing or transmission in and/or application programs used by telecom networks;
2.   Stealing or destroying others' information or harming other people's legal interests with telecom networks;
3.   Intentionally attacking telecom networks of others and other telecom facilities by making, copying, spreading computer viruses or other means;
4.   Engaging in other activities that would harm the security of telecom networks and information.

Article 59. No organization or individual is allowed to disturb the order of telecom markets by:

1.   Arbitrarily engaging in international, Hong Kong Special Administrative Region (HKSAR) and Macao Special Administrative Region (SAR) telecom businesses by leasing international telecom circuits, privately establishing adapted facilities or other means without authorization;
2.   Embezzling others' telecom lines, fabricating others' telecom codes and using knowingly copied or usurped telecom facilities and/or codes;
3.   Forging and falsifying telephone cards or other valued certificates of telecom services;
4.   Handling network-access formalities and using mobile phones with false or infringed identification cards.

Article 60. Telecom business operators should establish a complete internal security system and implement the responsibility system for telecom security in accordance with the State regulations on telecom security.

Article 61. Telecom business operators should design, construct, and operate their telecom networks completely in compliance with what are required by national security and telecom network security.

Article 62. When finding out that information transmitted through its own network in the course of its provision of public information services belongs to contents specified in Article 57 of this set of regulations, the telecom business operator concerned should stop the transmission of such information, keep the related record in custody and send corresponding reports to the related departments of the State immediately.

Article 63. Telecom users should be held liable for the contents of information that they transmit through the telecom networks as well as the consequences.

Where the information transmitted by the users falls within the scope of state secrets, confidential measures must be taken by the users concerned in transmission of the information according to the stipulations of confidential law of the State.

Article 64. In emergencies such as grave natural calamities, the department in charge of the information industry under the State Council shall, upon the approval of the State Council, be entitled to the right to transfer and use various kinds of telecom facilities to ensure the smooth operation of important communications.

Article 65. International communications businesses within the People's Republic of China should be conducted through the gateways of international communications established upon the approval of the department in charge of the information industry under the State Council.

Communications made between the Mainland China and HKSAR, Macao SAR and Taiwan should be conducted in reference to the stipulations of the previous clause.

Article 66. The freedom and privacy of telecom users in the legal use of telecom services shall be protected by law. No organization or individual is allowed to check the contents of telecommunications under whatever reason, except checks that are made by public security organizations, state security organizations or offices of the public prosecutors for the sake of national security or for tracking criminals.

Telecom business operators and their working staff are not allowed to provide contents of communications transmitted by subscribers through the telecom network to others without authorization.

CHAPTER SIX: PENALTIES

Article 67. Violators of Articles 57 and 58 shall be investigated by legal means where they have constituted crimes, and where the violation does not constitute a crime, shall be penalized by public or state security organizations in accordance with related laws and administrative regulations.

Article 68. Violators of the order of telecom markets by conducts listed in Clauses 2, 3 and 4 of Article 59 of this set of regulations shall be investigated for their criminal responsibilities where they are constituted as crimes, and where the violation does not constitute a crime, shall be requested by departments in charge of information under the State Council or telecom regulatory offices at the provincial level to rectify their acts and pay what they obtained illegally with a fine of three to five times the illegal income. Where there is no illegal income or that illegally obtained is less than RMB 10,000, a fine ranging from RMB 10,000 to RMB 100,000 shall be collected from the violators.

Article 69. Violators of this set of regulations by forging, infringement and transfer of permits to conduct telecom business, permits of telecom equipment for access to the network or by fabricating the serial numbers of network-access permits specified on telecom equipment shall have to pay for illegal income with a fine of three to five times the illegal income or pay a fine ranging from

RMB 10,000 to RMB 100,000 to the departments in charge of the information industry under the State Council or telecom regulatory offices at the provincial level according to authority of the departments.

Article 70. Violators of this set of regulations by having any of the following acts shall be requested by departments in charge of the information industry under the State Council or telecom regulatory offices at the provincial level according to the authority of the departments to rectify their acts and pay illegally obtained incomes with a fine of three to five times the illegal income or pay a fine ranging from RMB 100,000 to RMB 1 million where there is no illegal income or where the illegal income obtained is less than RMB 50,000. Violators in the following serious cases shall be requested to cease their business and undergo rectification:

1.   In violation of the stipulations of Clause 3 of Article 7 of this set of regulations or having done what is listed in Item 1 of Article 59 of this set of regulations by conducting telecom business without permission or conducting telecom business beyond the scope approved;
2.   Setting up an international communication gateway to conduct international communication business without approval from the department in charge of information industry under the State Council;
3.   Using, transferring and leasing telecom resources or changing the usage of telecom resources without authorization;
4.   Interrupting networks interconnection or access to service without authorization;
5.   Refusing to perform the universal service obligations.

Article 71. Violators of the stipulations of this set of regulations by conducting any of the following acts shall be requested by the department in charge of the information industry under the State Council or telecom regulatory offices at the provincial level to rectify the acts and pay what they have obtained illegally with a fine of one to three times the illegal income or a fine ranging from RMB 10,000 to RMB 100,000 where there is no illegal income or where the illegal income obtained is less than RMB 10,000. Violators of the following serious cases shall be requested to cease business and undergo rectification:

1.   Collecting extra charges in the course of interconnection between telecom networks in violation of the related stipulations;
2.   Failing to take effective measures to overcome the problems causing technical barriers between the networks;
3.   Providing contents of information transmitted by telecom users via the telecom network to others without permission by the users in question;
4.   Refusing to pay access charges of telecom resources as required.

Article 72. Violators of the stipulations of Article 42 of this set of regulations by having engaged in unfair competition in telecom operations shall be requested by departments in charge of the information industry under the State Council or telecom regulatory offices at the provincial level to rectify their acts and pay a fine ranging from RMB 100,000 to RMB 1 million. Violators whose acts are serious shall be requested to cease their business and undergo rectification.

Article 73. Violators of this set of regulations by having done any of the following acts shall be requested by departments in charge of information industry under the State Council or telecom regulatory offices at the provincial level to rectify their acts and pay a fine ranging from RMB 50,000 to RMB 500,000 according to the authority of the departments. Violators of the following serious cases shall be requested to cease their business and undergo rectification:

1.   Refusing requests for network interconnection proposed by other telecom operators;
2.   Refusing to enforce the decisions of network interconnections made in accordance to laws by departments in charge of information industry under the State Council or telecom regulatory offices at the provincial level;
3.   Quality of services provided to other telecom operators is inferior to those of its own networks and those provided to its affiliates or branches.

Article 74. Violators of the stipulations of Clause 1 of Article 34 and Clause 2 of Article 40 of this set of regulations by refusing to provide a list of fees for domestic long-distance calls, international calls, mobile communications, and information services, or refusing to provide local phone calls free of charge to telecom subscribers under dispute of fees charges of local phone calls shall be ordered by telecom regulatory offices at the provincial level to rectify their acts and apologize to the subscribers. Those who refuse to rectify their acts or offer their apologies shall be warned and fined between RMB 5,000 and RMB 50,000.

Article 75. Violators of the stipulations of Article 41 of this set of regulations shall be requested by telecom regulatory offices at the provincial level to rectify their acts, offer apologies, and make compensation to the telecom users via the telecom network and those who refuse to make rectification or compensation shall be warned and fined between RMB 10,000 and RMB 100,000. Violators whose acts are serious shall be requested to cease their business and undergo rectification.

Article 76. Violators of this set of regulations by having done any of the following acts shall be requested by telecom regulatory offices at the provincial level to rectify their acts and pay a fine ranging from RMB 10,000 to RMB 100,000. Violators whose acts are serious shall be requested to cease their business and undergo rectification:

1. Selling telecom terminal equipment that has no licence to access telecom networks;
2. Illegally preventing or hindering telecom operators from providing public telecom services to telecom users;
3. Changing or transferring telecom routes or other telecom facilities of others without permission.

Article 77. Violators of this set of regulations by lowering the quality and performance of products that have been granted permits to get access to telecom networks shall be penalized by departments supervising the quality of the products in accordance with the related laws and administrative regulations.

Article 78. Telecom business operators having committed any of the acts prohibited by Articles 57, 58 and 59 of this set of regulations will have their licences to conduct telecom business suspended by the original licence granting organizations where the cases are serious.

The department in charge of the information industry under the State Council or telecom regulatory offices at the provincial level shall inform the enterprise registration departments after their suspension of licences to the telecom business operators concerned.

Article 79. If employees of the department in charge of the information industry under the State Council or those of telecom regulatory offices at the provincial level are found guilty of misconduct in office, abuse of powers, favouritism and embezzlement that constitute crimes, their criminal responsibility shall be investigated in accordance with the laws. Those whose acts do not constitute crimes shall be meted out administrative penalties in accordance with the laws.

CHAPTER SEVEN: SUPPLEMENTARY ARTICLES

Article 80. Detailed rules on investment in the telecom sector by foreign institutions or individuals and those from Hong Kong SAR, Macao SAR and Taiwan in Mainland China shall be formulated separately by the State Council of the People's Republic of China.

Article 81. This set of regulations shall enter into force on the day of promulgation.

ANNEX: CATALOGUE OF THE CLASSIFICATION OF TELECOM BUSINESS

1.   Basic telecom business:

    a.   Domestic long distance calls and local calls of fixed telecom networks.

    b.   Mobile phone networks and data transmission.

    c.   Satellite communications and satellite mobile communicat- ions.

    d.   Internet and other public data transmission business.

    e.   Leasing or selling of bandwidth, wavelength, optical fibre, optical cable, tubing and other network elements.

    f.   Network support, access and leasing services.

    g.   International telecom infrastructure and international telecom business.

    h.   Wireless paging.

    i.   Resales of basic telecom business.

Business mentioned in (h) and (i) will be managed in reference to that of value-added telecom business.

2.   Value-added telecom business:

    a.   Email.

    b.   Voice mail.

    c.   Online databank service for information storage and retrieval.

    d.   Electronic data interchange (EDI).

    e.   Online data processing and transaction processing.

    f.   Value-added fax.

    g.   Internet access service.

    h.   Internet information service.

    i.   Video telephone conferencing service.

Note: Translated by the authors from www.mii.cn/news2000/1013_1.htm.

Appendix 3. Regulations on foreign-invested telecom enterprises

(Promulgated by the Ministry of Information Industry on 11 December 2001; reported by Xinhua News Agency on 20 December 2001)

Article 1. These regulations are enacted according to the laws and administrative regulations related to foreign investment and the Regulations on Telecommunications of the People's Republic of China (hereinafter referred to as the Telecom Regulations) in order to meet the needs of opening up the telecom sector and promoting the development of the telecom sector.

Article 2. A foreign-invested telecom enterprise is an enterprise that is founded according to law in the form of a Chinese-foreign joint venture by foreign and Chinese investors within the territory of the People's Republic of China and provides telecom services.

Article 3. While conducting telecom business operations, foreign-invested telecom enterprises must observe the provisions of the Telecom Regulations and other related laws and administrative regulations, in addition to these new regulations.

Article 4. Foreign-invested telecom enterprises may provide basic and value-added telecom services. The categorization of specific business shall be in compliance with the provisions of the Telecom Regulations. The department in charge of the information industry under the State Council shall determine the geographic range for the business of foreign-invested telecom enterprises according to related regulations.

Article 5. The registered capital of foreign-invested telecom enterprises shall conform to the following provisions:

1. Those providing basic telecom services across the country or across provinces, autonomous regions and municipalities shall have no less than RMB 2 billion (US$ 241.55 million) in registered capital.

2.   Those providing value-added telecom services shall have no less than RMB 10 million (US$ 1.21 million) in registered capital.
3.   Those providing basic telecom services in provinces, autonomous regions and municipalities shall have no less than RMB 200 million (US$ 24.15 million) in registered capital. Those providing value-added telecom services shall have no less than RMB 1 million (US$ 120,773) in registered capital.

Article 6. In foreign-invested telecom enterprises that provide basic telecom services (excluding paging services), the contribution by the foreign party shall be no more than 49 per cent.

In foreign-invested telecom enterprises that provide value-added telecom services (including paging in basic telecom services), the contribution by the foreign party shall be no more than 50 per cent.

The department in charge of the information industry under the State Council shall determine, according to related provisions, the percentage of contribution by foreign and Chinese investors to a foreign-invested telecom enterprise in different periods.

Article 7. While conducting telecom business, foreign-invested telecom enterprises shall meet requirements as stipulated in the Telecom Regulations for providing basic and value-added telecom services, in addition to requirements stipulated in Articles 4, 5 and 6 of these regulations.

Article 8. The major Chinese investor in a foreign-invested telecom enterprise that provides basic telecom services shall meet the following requirements:

1.   Be a company founded according to law;
2.   Have enough funding and staff to run the operations; and
3.   Meet the requirements stipulated by the department in charge of the information industry under the State Council for prudent and special sectors.

The major Chinese investor in a foreign-invested telecom enterprise mentioned in this article refers to the one that makes the largest contribution among all the Chinese investors, which accounts for more than 30 per cent of the total contribution by all the Chinese investors.

Article 9. The major foreign investor in a foreign-invested telecom enterprise that provides basic telecom services shall meet the following requirements:

1.   Be qualified to be a 'legal person' of the enterprise;

2. Have a business licence for basic telecom services in the country or region where it is registered;
3. Have enough funding and staff to run the operations; and
4. Have a good track record regarding performance and operational experience in basic telecom services.

The major foreign investor in a foreign-invested telecom enterprise mentioned in this article refers to the one that makes the largest contribution among all the foreign investors, which accounts for more than 30 per cent of the total contribution by the foreign investors.

Article 10. The major foreign investor in a foreign-invested telecom enterprise that provides value-added telecom services shall have a good track record regarding performance and operational experience in value-added telecom services.

Article 11. To set up a foreign-invested telecom enterprise that provides basic or value-added telecom services across provinces, autonomous regions and municipalities, the major Chinese investor shall apply to the department in charge of the information industry under the State Council and submit the following documents:

1. Project proposal;
2. Feasibility study;
3. Qualification certificates or relevant confirmation documents of all the investors as stipulated in Articles 8, 9 and 10 of these regulations; and
4. Certificates or confirmation documents for other qualifications as stipulated in the Telecom Regulations for providing basic or value-added telecom services.

The department in charge of the information industry under the State Council shall examine the aforementioned relevant documents after receiving the application.

For basic telecom services, the examination shall be completed in 180 days with the decision of approval or disapproval.

For value-added telecom services, the examination shall be completed in 90 days with the decision of approval or disapproval. If the application is approved, the Written Opinion on the Examination and Approval of Telecom Services Involving Foreign Investment will be issued.

If the application is not approved, the applicant will be notified in written form and given the reason.

Article 12. When applying for setting up a foreign-invested telecom enterprise to provide basic telecom services or value-added telecom services across provinces, autonomous regions and municipalities according to provisions in Article 11 of these regulations, the major Chinese investor may submit other documents first before submitting the feasibility study.

It may submit the feasibility study report after receiving the written approval notice from the department in charge of the information industry under the State Council. But the interval between the date of the approval notice and the date of submitting the feasibility study report shall be no more than 12 months.

Moreover, this interval is not counted in the stipulated examination and approval period.

Article 13. To set up a foreign-invested telecom enterprise that provides value-added telecom services in provinces, autonomous regions and municipalities, the major Chinese investor shall apply to the provincial, regional or municipal telecom authority and submit the following documents:

1.   Project proposal;
2.   Qualification certificates or relevant confirmation documents as stipulated in Article 10 of these regulations; and
3.   Certificates or confirmation documents for other qualifications as stipulated in the Telecom Regulations for providing value-added telecom services.

The provincial, regional or municipal telecom authority shall make a decision in 60 days after receiving the application. If the application is approved, it shall be resubmitted to the department in charge of the information industry under the State Council.

If the application is not approved, the applicant shall be notified in written form and given the reason.

The department in charge of the information industry under the State Council shall complete the examination-and-approval procedures and make a decision within 30 days of receiving the application documents approved by the provincial, regional or municipal telecom authority.

If the application is approved, the Written Opinion on the Examination and Approval of Telecom Services Involving Foreign Investment will be issued. If the application is not approved, the applicant shall be notified in written form and given the reason.

Article 14. The project proposal of a foreign-invested telecom enterprise shall mainly include names of all parties concerned and their basic information, the total investment and registered capital of the enterprise to be set up, percentage of contribution by parties concerned, the type of business to be engaged in, the terms of joint venture, etc.

The feasibility study of a foreign-invested telecom enterprise shall mainly include the basic information of the enterprise to be set up, its service items, business forecast and development plans, analysis of return on investment, anticipated operation period, etc.

Article 15. While setting up a foreign-invested telecom enterprise, if, according to relevant state regulations, the investment project needs the examination and approval of the planning department of the State Council or the economic comprehensive administration department of the State Council, the department in charge of the information industry under the State Council shall resubmit the application documents to the planning department of the State Council or the economic comprehensive administration department of the State Council for examination and approval before issuing the Written Opinion on the Examination and Approval of Telecom Services Involving Foreign Investment.

For projects resubmitted to the planning department of the State Council or the economic comprehensive administration department of the State Council for examination and approval, the examination-and-approval period stipulated in Articles 11 and 13 of these regulations may be extended for another 30 days.

Article 16. If the foreign-invested telecom enterprise is to provide basic telecom services or value-added telecom services across provinces, autonomous regions and municipalities, the major Chinese investor shall, with the Written Opinion on the Examination and Approval of Telecom Services Involving Foreign Investment, submit the contracts and articles of the foreign-invested telecom enterprise to be set up to the department in charge of foreign trade and economic cooperation under the State Council.

If the enterprise is to provide value-added telecom services in provinces, autonomous regions and municipalities, the major Chinese investor shall, with the Written Opinion on the Examination and Approval of Telecom Services Involving Foreign Investment, submit the contracts and articles of the foreign-invested telecom enterprise to be set up to the department in charge of foreign trade and economic cooperation under the provincial, regional or municipal people's government.

The department in charge of foreign trade and economic cooperation under the State Council and the department in charge of foreign trade and economic cooperation under the provincial, regional or municipal people's government shall complete the examination of the contracts and articles of the foreign-invested telecom enterprise to be set up and make the decision of approval or disapproval within 90 days of receiving them.

In case of approval, the Certificate of Approval for Foreign-invested Enterprises will be issued. In case of disapproval, the applicant will be notified in written form and given the reason.

Article 17. With the Certificate of Approval for Foreign-invested Enterprises, the major Chinese investor of the foreign-invested telecom enterprise shall obtain the Business Licence for Telecom Services at the department in charge of the information industry under the State Council.

With the Certificate of Approval for Foreign-invested Enterprises and the Business Licence for Telecom Services, the major Chinese investor of the foreign-invested telecom enterprise shall register the foreign-invested telecom enterprise at the department for industrial and commercial administration.

Article 18. A foreign-invested telecom enterprise intending to provide cross-border telecom services must obtain the approval of the department in charge of the information industry under the State Council.

The services shall be provided through an international telecom exit and entry bureau set up with the approval of the department in charge of the information industry under the State Council.

Article 19. As for violators of Article 6 of these regulations, the department in charge of the information industry under the State Council shall order them to make amends within a given period, plus pay a fine of between RMB 100,000 (US$ 12,077) and RMB 500,000 (US$ 60,386).

If a violator fails to make amends before the specified date, the department in charge of the information industry under the State Council shall revoke the Business Licence for Telecom Services, and the department in charge of foreign trade and economic cooperation shall cancel the Certificate of Approval for Foreign-invested Enterprises it issued.

Article 20. As for violators of Article 18 of these regulations, the department in charge of the information industry under the State Council shall order them to make amends within a given period, plus pay a fine of between RMB 200,000 (US$ 24,155) and RMB 1 million (US$ 120,773).

If a violator fails to make amends before the specified date, the department in charge of the information industry under the State Council shall revoke the Business Licence for Telecom Services, and the department in charge of foreign trade and economic cooperation shall cancel the Certificate of Approval for Foreign-invested Enterprises it issued.

Article 21. If the application for setting up a foreign-invested telecom enterprise is approved through providing false and fake qualification certificates or confirmation documents, the approval will be deemed invalid.

Moreover, the department in charge of the information industry under the State Council shall impose a fine of between RMB 200,000 (US$ 24,155) and RMB 1 million (US$ 120,773) and revoke the Business Licence for Telecom Services, while the department in charge of foreign trade and economic cooperation shall cancel the Certificate of Approval for Foreign-invested Enterprises it issued.

Article 22. Foreign-invested telecom enterprises that violate the provisions of the Telecom Regulations and other related laws and administrative regulations shall be penalized according to law by relevant authorities.

Article 23. A domestic telecom enterprise that intends to be listed overseas must apply to the department in charge of the information industry under the State Council for examination and approval according to relevant state regulations.

Article 24. These regulations are applicable to corporations and enterprises from the Hong Kong Special Administrative Region, the Macau Special Administrative Region and Taiwan that invest in and provide telecom services on the mainland.

Article 25. These regulations shall go into effect on Jan. 1, 2002.

Bibliography

BOOKS AND ARTICLES

Becker, Jasper (2002), 'Princes of privatisation reign', *South China Morning Post*, 10 January.

Dai, Quanming (2002), '*Xiaolingtong re de leng sikao*' (Cool thoughts on PHS boom), *Youdian Jingji* [*P & T Economy* (Shanghai)], **58**, 19–22.

Deng, L.Q., Ma, H. and Wu, H. (1993), *Dangdai Zhongguo de Youdian Shiye* (*Contemporary China's Posts and Telecommunications Industry*), Beijing: Contemporary China Publisher.

Eglin, Richard (2003), 'Challenges and implications of China joining the WTO: what WTO accession means', in Ding Lu, G. J. Wen and H. Zhou (eds), *China's Economic Globalization through the WTO*, Aldershot: Ashgate, pp. 173–225.

Gao, Chao (2002), '*Xiaolingtong reng you fazhan kongjian*' (PHS still has potentials), *Youdian Jingji* [*P & T Economy* (Shanghai)], **59**, 16–19.

Gao, Yangzhi (1991) (in Chinese), '*Shanghai dianhua wang de fazhan xianzhuang he fazhan zhanlue*' (Shanghai's telephone network: status quo and development strategy), *Youdian Jingji* [*P & T Economy* (Shanghai)], **16**, 22–28.

Gao, Yangzhi (2001) (in Chinese), '*Guanyu Dianxin Longduan de renshi wuqu shi-er ti*' (On twelve misunderstandings of telecom monopoly: views against divestiture of China Telecom), *Youdian Jingji* [*P & T Economy* (Shanghai)], **56**, 9–19.

Gao, Yangzhi (2002) (in Chinese), '*Lun ru shi' hou dianxinye de shichang fengxian he zhidu fengxian*' (On telecom sector's market risks and institutional risks after accession the WTO), *Youdian Jingji* [*P & T Economy* (Shanghai)], **59**, 3–9.

Gao, Ping and Lyytinen, Kalle (2000), 'Transformation of China's telecommunications sector: A market perspective', *Telecommunications Policy*, **24**, 719–730.

Guo, R.C. and Xu, Yan (1992), *Business Accounting System for Postal and Telecommunications Enterprises*, Beijing: Beijing University of Posts and Telecommunications Press.

He, Fei Chang (1994), 'Lian Tong: a quantum leap in the reform of China's telecommunications', *Telecommunications Policy*, **18** (3), 206–210.

Hong, Xiuyi and Qian, Yongwei (1992) (in Chinese), '*Woguo chengshi zhuzhai dianhua fazhan qushi yu sikao*' (The trend of residential telephone development in China), *Youdian Jingji* [*P & T Economy* (Shanghai)], **21** (4), 19–23.

Hsu, Connie (1999), *Telecoms & Wireless Asia*, London: The Economist Intelligence Unit.

International Telecommunications Union (ITU) (1995), *Yearbook of Statistics: Telecommunications Services Chronological Time Series*, Geneva: ITU.

International Telecommunications Union (ITU) (2001), *Yearbook of Statistics: Telecommunications Services Chronological Time Series*, Geneva: ITU.

Jin, Jiyuan (1992) (in Chinese), '*Shenhua gaige, zhuanhuan qiye jingying jizhi jige wenti de tantao*' (Issues of deepening reform of enterprise operational rules), *Youdian Jingji* [*P & T Economy* (Shanghai)], **20** (4), 4–6.

Jing Xing (1999) (in Chinese), '*Jianchi shishi qiushi, yiqie cong shij chufa – wei jinian gaige kaifa 20 zhounian zuo*' (Insist on the principle of pragmatism – on the 20th anniversary of the commencement of reform and opening), *Youdian Jingji* [*P & T Economy* (Shanghai)], **46** (1), 2–8.

Johnson, D. Gale (1998), 'China's great famine: introductory remarks', *China Economic Review*, **9** (2), 103–110.

Li, Jiaju (2000) (in Chinese), '*Waixiang ershiyi shiji de zhongguo liudong dianhua shichang*' (China's mobile telephone market towards the 21st century), *Youdian Jingji* [*P & T Economy* (Shanghai)] **50** (1), 14–19.

Li, Jinshan (1998), 'Bureaucratic restructure in reforming China: a redistribution of political power', *EAI Occasional Paper No. 9*, The East Asian Institute, National University of Singapore.

Lin, Justin Y., Cai, F. and Li, Z. (1996), *The China Miracle: Development Strategy and Economic Reform*, Hong Kong: The Chinese University Press.

Lin, Sun (2000), 'Exploring new avenues: Unicom's focus on growth', *Asian Communications*, August **14** (8), 12.

Liu, Zhaoquan (1992) (in Chinese), '*Youdian fazhan yu chanquan guanli tizhi gaige*' (The development of P & T and reform of asset management), *Youdian Jingji* [*P & T Economy* (Shanghai)], **18** (1), 2–4.

Lu, Ding (1994), 'The management of China's telecommunications industry: some institutional facts', *Telecommunications Policy*, **18** (3), 195–205.

Lu, Ding (2000), 'China's telecommunications infrastructure buildup: on its own way', in Takatoshi Ito and Anne O. Krueger (eds), *Deregulation and*

Interdependence in the Asia-Pacific Region,   Chicago: University of Chicago Press, pp. 371–414.

Ma, Qiang (1992) (in Chinese), '*Dianxin zifei de pingjia fangfa ji guoji bijiao*' (Ways to estimate telecommunications rates and an international comparison of rates), *Youdian Jingji* [*P & T Economy* (Shanghai)], **18** (1), 27–30.

Ministry of Information Industry (2001), 'Summary of the Tenth Five-year Plan (2001–2005) – Information Industry', http://www.mii.gov.cn/.

McKibbin, Warwick J. and Woo, Wing Thye (2003), 'The Consequences of China's WTO Accession on its Neighbours', *Asian Economic Papers*, **2** (2), http://www.econ.ucdavis.edu/faculty/woo/woo.html.

Mueller, Milton and Lovelock, Peter (2000), 'The WTO and China's ban on foreign investment in telecommunications services: a game-theoretic analysis', *Telecommunications Policy*, **24** (2000), 731–759.

Mueller, Milton and Tan, Zixiang (1997), *China in the Information Age: Telecommunications and the Dilemma of Reform*, Westport, CT: Praeger Publishers.

Qian, Jinqun and Zhang, Yi (2000), '*Jin nian lai woguo dianxin zifei tiaozheng qingkuang*' (Adjustment of telecommunications rates in the recent years), *Dianxin Ruan Kexue Yuanjiu* (*Telecom Soft Science Research*), (3), 28–37.

Rothman, Warren H. and Barker, Jonathan P. (1999), 'Cable connections', *The China Business Review* (US), **26** (3), 20–25.

Sun, Yaming (1992) (in Chinese), '*Youdian xin yewu zifei zhengce youguan wenti de tantao*' (Issues related to pricing policies regarding P & T new services), *Youdian Jingji* [*P & T Economy* (Shanghai)], **18** (1), 36–37.

Tan,   Zixiang   (1994),   'Challenges   to   the   MPT's   monopoly', *Telecommunications Policy*, **18** (3), 174–181.

Tan, Zixiang (1999), 'Regulating China's Internet: convergence toward a coherent regulatory regime' *Telecommunications Policy*, **23** (3–4), 261–276.

Ure, John (1994), 'Telecommunications, with Chinese characteristics', *Telecommunications Policy*, **18** (3), 182–194.

Wan, Lijiang (2001), '*Ge pai piyi longzheng hudou*' (Conflicts of interests), *21shiji jingji baodao* (*21st Century Economic News*), 31 December.

Wang, Jiang-yu (2001), 'The Internet and e-commerce in China: regulations, judicial views, and government policies', *Computer and Internet Lawyer* (Frederick), **18** (1), 12–30.

Wong, Chee Kong (2002), 'China's telecommunications: industrial policy with "Chinese" characteristics', Thesis submitted for the degree of Master of Social Sciences, National University of Singapore.

Wong, John and Nah, S.L., (2000), 'Internet in China', *EAI Background Brief No. 63*, East Asian Institute, National University of Singapore.

Woo, Wing Thye (2001), 'Recent claims of China's economic exceptionalism: reflections inspired by WTO accession', *China Economic Review* (US), **12** (2/3), 107–136.

Wu, Jichuan (2000) (in Chinese), 'Interview on reform and opening of the telecommunications sector', *Youdian Jingji* [*P & T Economy* (Shanghai)], **50** (1), 2–4.

Xiao, Geng and Zhou, Fang (2000), 'WTO and China's economic transformation: institutional perspectives and policy options', in Lau Chung-ming and Jianfa Shen (eds), *China Review 2000*, Hong Kong: The Chinese University Press, pp. 209–222

Xu, Yan (1996), 'Competition without privatization: the Chinese path', Paper presented at the Eleventh Biennial Conference of the International Telecommunications Society, Seville, Spain, 19 June.

Yang, Peifang (1991) (in Chinese), '*Lun dianxin hangye de mubiao he xietiao fazhan*' (On the goals and ways of a harmonic development of telecommunication), *Youdian Jingji* [*P & T Economy* (Shanghai)], **16** (3), 2–4.

You, Zhengyan (1987), 'Status of postal and telecommunications sector and industrial policies', in *Yearbook of China Transportation and Communications*, Beijing: China Transportation and Communications Society, pp. 766–768.

Zhang, Xuan (1991), 'A discussion of perfecting the economic mechanism of telecommunications enterprises', *Youdian Jingji* [*P & T Economy* (Shanghai)], **16** (3), pp. 5–7.

Zhang, Lianshun and Fang, Wu (eds) (1994) (in Chinese), *A Practical Guide to New Tax Laws*, Beijing: China Development Publishing House.

Zhou, He (1997), 'A history of telecommunications in China: development and policy implications', in Paul S.N. Lee (ed.), *Telecommunications and development in China*, New Jersey: Hampton Press, pp. 55–87.

Zhou, Qiren (2001), 'Wei shichang zhongzu liu you kongjian: guanyu zhongguo dianxin de zaici chaifen' (Leaving room for market restructure: on China Telecom's second divestiture), http://www.ccer.edu.cn/.

Zhou Zhiqun (1991), 'The usage of foreign investment in P & T business', *Youdian Jingji* [*P & T Economy* (Shanghai)], **16** (3), 36–37.

Zhu, Rongji (2000), 'On the drawing of the Tenth Five-year Plan', *People's Daily*, 20 October.

MAIN STATISTICAL SOURCES

China Transportation and Communications Society (various years), *Zhongguo Jiaotong Nianjian* (*Yearbook of China Transportation and Communications*), Beijing: Year Book House of China Transportation and Communications.

Ministry of Finance (various years), *Zhongguo Caizheng Nianjian* (*Yearbook of China's Public Finance*), Beijing: China Fiscal Press.

Ministry of Foreign Trade and Economic Cooperation (various years), *Almanac of China's Foreign Economic Relations*, Beijing: Foreign Trade and Economic Cooperation Press.

State Statistics Bureau (various years), *China Statistical Yearbook*, Beijing: China Statistics Press.

World Bank (various years), *World Development Report*, Washington, DC: World Bank.

Index

access to network 53–4
  see also network
  interconnection and charges 97, 103–5
  internet 47, 49, 54, 89, 101
  regulation 64
accounting system
  MPT reorganization and 21
  rules reform 23
agreement
  Sino-European, on China's WTO
    entry 79
  Sino-US, on China's accession to
    WTO, timetable for opening
    market 80
Alcatel Shanghai Bell 90
Approval (for license or project)
  application for, *Regulations on*
    Foreign-Invested Telecom
    Enterprises (Articles 8 and 9) 87
  international transmission network,
    Provisions of Telecom Network
    Construction (Article 20) 88
  MII procedures 87–8
  review-and-approval process,
    Provisions of Telecom Network
    Construction (Article 17) 88
AT&T 44, 72, 90, 97
  -Bell group 33,
Australia
  foreign direct investment and 90

Barker, Jonathan P. 54, 61
Becker, Jasper 98
broadband
  network development, regulatory
    framework and 53–5
bureaux of post and telecom (PTB)
  financial incentives and 23–4
  fixed capital investment and 28
  MPT reorganization and 21
  State support and 24

business
  interests 37–9, 55, 60–63, 74, 81, 83,
    91, 94, 98, 101, 104–5, 110
  scope of six major carriers
    (2001) 49
    (after May 2002) 101
  state share in telecom business,
    Telecommunications Regulations
    2000 and 84

capital
  see also financial incentives; fixed
    capital investment
  construction investment and profit of
    postal and telecom enterprises 20
  fixed 27–30
  minimum registered, licensing and
    approval procedures and 87
capital construction investment
  postal and telecom enterprises profit
    and 20
carriers
  business scope of
    (2001) 49
    (after May 2002) 101
  indigenous, listing overseas 82–3
  market shares of
    (2001) 95
    (first half of 2000) 48
China *see* People's Republic of China
Chinese Academy of Science 37, 47, 54
China Mobile 45, 48–9, 53, 56–9, 81–3,
    94–5, 99, 101–5
China Netcom (later China Netcom
    Communication Group
    Corporation)
  entry 54–6, 58, 61, 63
  foreign capital and 82, 93, 96
  market share 95
  MII guided competition and 47–8, 49
  second-tier interest group and 97